PASTOR'S PILGRIMAGE

KEITH FORECAST

PASTOR'S PILGRIMAGE

The memoirs of a twentieth century Christian minister

'The boundary lines have fallen for me in pleasant places; I have a goodly heritage'.
Psalm 16.6 (NRSV)

Matador
9 De Montfort Mews
Leicester LE1 7FW, UK
Tel: (+44) 116 255 9311 / 9312
Email: books@troubador.co.uk
Web: www.troubador.co.uk/matador

ISBN 978-1906510-367

A Cataloguing-in-Publication (CIP) catalogue record for this book
is available from the British Library.

Mixed Sources
Product group from well-managed
forests and other controlled sources
www.fsc.org Cert no. TT-COC-2082
© 1996 Forest Stewardship Council

Typeset in 11pt Bembo by Troubador Publishing Ltd, Leicester, UK
Printed in the UK by The Cromwell Press Ltd, Trowbridge, Wilts, UK

Matador is an imprint of Troubador Publishing Ltd

I dedicate this memoir to those who have shared my life most intimately:
to my children – Stephen, Rebekah, Christopher and Judith
who have had to put up with me throughout their lives;

to their children – Connor, Naomi, Stella, Sahara and Beaufort
who are a great delight and might find something of interest here in years
to come;

and above all to the memory of my wife Frances,
hoping she realised how much I owed to her in all my life and ministry
during the forty years of our partnership.

Thanks

I am grateful to all whose memories have prompted my own and enabled me
to write this account of my life and experience. In particular I am grateful to
my friends Jim and Jill Hollyman of Bolton who have read the script
and made valuable comments and suggestions.

FOREWORD

Why do people write their autobiographies? What makes them think other people might be remotely interested in their lives? Is this not the height of arrogance? Why do they do it – and why am I doing it now? It is not that I think my story is specially important, or that I have any special claim to be remembered. I am fully aware that in a few years' time my life will be forgotten except perhaps among my family and friends. The book began with a suggestion by members of my family for some kind of record, so I am dedicating the book to them. Furthermore, I have lived through one of the most turbulent centuries the world has ever known, and for forty-eight years I have served as a minister of the Church during a highly significant period of its history. Perhaps, therefore, my story might be of interest, not merely for its own sake but for what it reveals about its context. Thus I feel an urge to share it.

I have been fortunate – immensely fortunate. I am aware that life has smiled upon me for the most part, and that I have experienced far more of its good things than I have deserved. 'The boundary lines have indeed fallen for me in pleasant places'. To the God who gave me life and to all who have walked with me and shared my experience, I offer this account as an act of humble gratitude.

Chapter 1
ONCE UPON A TIME – 1935-1939

'This is my story', as the old Sankey revivalist hymn says. It begins in 1935. But does it? Mr story, like everyone's story, has roots that go far back into history.

I come from working class origins on both sides of the family. My father, George Alfred Forecast, was born in 1898, the only child of George and Elizabeth Forecast who at that time were living in rooms in Homerton, now part of the London Borough of Hackney. He has told his story in an unpublished memoir entitled 'Former Days – a Spiritual Pilgrimage', a treasured copy of which is on my desk as I write. The early part of that memoir in particular gives a fascinating picture of life in a very different world. He tells how his mother sang him war songs during the South African war of 1899-1902; how his father earned 18 shillings a week (approximately 90p in today's money) and how he often had to 'moonlight' to make ends meet. He also tells how he befriended a lad at school, very sparsely and poorly clad in the cold weather, shared his lunch with him, and went home with him to find him living in a dark basement room with sacks on the floor for rugs. The whole experience made him appreciate both the needs of people less fortunate than himself and his own family's comparatively good fortune. His story also tells of his days in the Grove Mission Sunday School attached to Clapton Park Congregational Church, then a large flourishing congregation. The Sunday School had over 700 scholars at the time, and the mother church had over 600 members. The Mission Hall closed during the second world war and the church, which still worships in its huge Victorian building (listed, of course!), now records 37 members. A different world indeed.

The Forecast family tree can be traced back to Huguenot immigrants who came to England from France when Louis XIV revoked the Edict of Nantes in 1685, bringing to an end a significant period of religious toleration in France and making life impossible for Protestants. Many of them came to East London, settling in Shoreditch and Hackney. Mostly they worked as clothiers, milliners and printers. Among them came a couple with the name of 'Forques'. Gradually, through usage, this name mutated through 'Forquest' to Forecast, and Forecast it has remained.

There have never been many of us; we all appear to derive from that one immigrant family; and to this day all those who share our family name either still live in North East London and its environs or can trace their history back to that part of the world.

My paternal great-grandfather was George Forecast – there was at least one George in the family throughout the 19th Century. He was a soldier in the Indian Army, and I have in my possession a number of papers relating to him and his family, including his army pass-book: a very interesting document. He enlisted in the army on January 27 1860 at the age of 20. His birth-place is given as Bethnal Green in the County of Middlesex (that was where it was then: inner London now!) and his trade is recorded as 'Labourer'. His wife, whom he married in 1871, was his first cousin, called Caroline, and he had three children: Caroline, George and Eliza. He died in 1883 at the age of 43, leaving his wife very poor: there is a record of her earning seven shillings a week in 1884 by cleaning a church. This is my humble ancestry on my father's side.

My grandfather, also George, was originally in the printing trade, working for some of the large printing houses in the City of London: Hazell, Watson and Viney, Waterlow and Sons, Cassell. Thus, over 200 years after the Huguenot immigration, here was a descendant of those first settlers still employed in a trade which was common among his ancestors. Moreover, the family still lived in Hackney!

I remember my Grandpa Forecast as a quiet, gentle man, living a simple life, working at the time I first remember him for the Letchworth firm of Shelvoke and Drury, manufacturers of refuse vehicles. After his retirement during the Second World War he contented himself with his garden, his workshop and his dog – Tess, an obese wire-haired terrier. When not thus engaged he sat in his favourite chair in the living room, smoking his pipe and listening either to the radio or to scratched records played on his ancient wind-up gramophone. He had little conversation, but a twinkle in his eye which endeared him to my brother and me. It amused us that, when we went to visit, the first thing he'd say, almost before we had got in through the door, was 'What time is your train home?'! The other characteristic I remember, after all these years, is the smell of 'Erinmore' tobacco on his large bushy moustache. I hated being kissed by him! He died of throat and mouth cancer, in 1957.

Keith aged 1

Grandma Forecast was a stronger character. Like my grandfather, she tended to keep herself to herself, but she made her presence felt. She had a strong Christian faith, to which my father attributes his own Christian commitment. Her faith was, perhaps inevitably, of the unquestioning Victorian kind, with a somewhat judgmental God and a keen sense of right and wrong. She was a confirmed Anglican, though when I remember her she rarely attended church. Her interests lay in maintaining her simple home, caring for her husband, taking a deep interest in the family – and gossiping about her neighbours! She spent a good deal of time standing inside her living room window, peering out between the curtains to see what these neighbours were doing! Though five years older than her husband, she outlived him by three years, dying in 1960 at the age of 90. I treasure still the sideboard she left me in her will, together with its contents. She also left me £50 which, as Frances and I were married in the year she died, we spent on our first gas cooker.

My mother Annie, always known as Nancy, was one of nine children, born at roughly two-yearly intervals to William and Caroline Goulding who lived in Longton in the Staffordshire Potteries. Grandpa Goulding was a potter: a sagger-maker to be specific. Saggers were the rough clay containers into which fine china-clay crockery was packed and sealed before being fired in the coal ovens of the time. He started work with the fine bone china firm, Shelleys, at the age of 12 in 1882 and continued in the same post until he retired in 1940 when he was 70. Two of his sons, Bill and George, worked for the same firm. He was, in his way, a talented musician, though circumstances had prevented him from developing the talent as he would have liked. He conducted the choir of the Methodist Church to which he and his family belonged, and was also the conductor of another choir, which I believe he had formed, called the Pottery Workers' Choir. I still have his full score of 'The Messiah' by Handel, which was a regular part of the repertoire of these choirs, together with a number of other oratorio scores of his. I remember him thumping out tunes on his piano (he had been self-taught) and singing at the top of his tenor voice, both at home and in church. He also owned and played a concertina in the days when these were popular – I believe my brother has his instrument still. He was a little man, not much more than five feet tall, and had very decided views which he expounded at length to anyone who would listen, and to some who might have preferred not to listen! Like my paternal grandfather, he was a pipe-smoker. He was a tireless talker, and it is amusing to remember how he would hold his loaded pipe in one hand and his lighted match in the other, often failing to bringing the two together while he continued talking and letting the match burn down to his fingers! Another memory is of the way he hung his trousers right up under his armpits on braces, the buckles of which were slid over on to his back, this reducing them to their shortest extent! He outlived my grandmother by ten years, and used to come to stay with us by train. He had always met someone interesting on the train – and we often wondered what stories those people told, when they arrived at their destination, about the old man they had met who wouldn't stop talking! He died in 1956 at the age of 86.

I remember Grandma Goulding well even though I was only 11 when she died. She was a patient, caring person, strong in character but less impetuous than her husband. My mother told many stories about her mother. One that lingers in my memory was how Grandma would tie her daughters' hair with yellow ribbons every time there was an election – yellow, the colour of the Liberal Party to which she and her husband had given their life-time allegiance – and that was at a time when women did not yet have the vote! Grandma was also a member of the British Women's Total Abstinence Union, with its badge of a 'little white ribbon'. She was fiercely tee-total, a stance she had derived from her childhood experience of the habitual drunkenness of her own father, who spent most of his weekly pay on drink on the way home on Thursdays (pay-day) and then made great show of singing in the chapel choir on Sundays. One can therefore understand her attitude, one which she communicated to all her own children and which my own parents maintained throughout their lives.

Mother came in the middle of the large Goulding family. The youngest boy, Harold, born in 1918, died at the age of seven, a victim of scarlet fever – a prevalent scourge in those days. The other brothers and sisters all lived into adulthood. What I lacked of aunts and uncles on my father's side, he being an only child, I thus made up for on my mother's side. In ascending order of age, they were Muriel, a professional cook, Charles (Charlie), a school teacher, William (Bill), a potter, Nancy, my mother, George, also a potter, Millicent (Millie), a secretary, Harry, first a sailor in the Navy and later an Anglican priest and Naval chaplain, and Mary Beatrice (Beattie), a secretary. Two of the four daughters (Beattie and Millie) and one of the five sons (George) never left the family home, and Grandma cared for them as they went about their chosen careers. She was responsible for the cleaning and cooking, in the traditional manner, right up to the time of her death. One incident I recall with a smile took place one Good Friday towards the end of the war when we were staying in their house for the weekend. Though a staunch Methodist, she always insisted on having fish for lunch on Good Friday. She set off at 9.00 to buy it on this particular day – and arrived home at about 1.30, having had to search for it from shop to shop and to queue for hours when she did finally find some on sale. Such was wartime restriction, and such was my grandmother's determination.

Grandma Goulding's Methodism also reveals another interesting feature. Methodist Churches are grouped in Circuits and each circuit has a 'Plan' which lists all the preachers in all the churches for each quarter of the year. Thus it is possible to know, before setting out for church, who will be leading the worship on that particular occasion, and a good many people would stay away when certain people were scheduled to preach. Grandma always refused to have a copy of the plan in her house. 'I go to church to worship God' she declared, 'not to admire the preacher'. I wonder if these attitudes still pertain? Grandma was an example to all worshippers, Methodist or otherwise. She died on a Sunday night in 1947, aged 74, sitting at home with Grandpa at the side of the open fire, listening to 'Sunday Half-Hour' and reading the 'Methodist Recorder'. Her death was the first experience I had of bereavement, and it has affected my attitude to death ever since.

It is worth recording that both my sets of Grandparents lived to celebrate their Golden Weddings – the Gouldings in 1945 and the Forecasts in 1947. I have the photographs to prove it. It was rare in those days for people to reach this milestone and even rarer for families to have all four grandparents living to do so.

I have a faint memory of my Great-Grandma Goulding – Grandpa's mother. She died in 1938 at the age of 93, so she must have been born in 1845. What a link with the past! My one memory of her is of a visit I paid with my mother. Great-Grandma was sitting up in bed wearing a blue bed-jacket. That's all I remember, but photographs show her to be a very small lady, less than five feet tall, clad in the long black dress favoured by Victorian widows and a black bonnet.

My father was a gentle, sensitive person, approachable and sympathetic – a blend of the personalities of both his parents. Sadly, they could not afford for him to continue at school beyond the age of 14 and he failed to pass the scholarship examination that would have qualified him for grammar school and education through to 18. He always regretted that, as a result, some doors were not open to him – doors which swung on their hinges for my generation with the advent of universal free education through school to university. I knew he took delight in the opportunities, denied to him, that came to his two sons.

Before the war he worked as a clerk for the solicitors' firm Simmonds and Simmonds in the City of London. I believe the company still exists – it did a few years ago. The office was in Threadneedle Street, at the side of the Royal Exchange. He liked to tell how in 1912, very early in his time in that office, he watched the funeral procession of General Booth of the Salvation Army go past. In my early childhood my father travelled to his London office daily by train from Letchworth where we then lived – a journey that probably took him about an hour each way. Even then commuting from distant parts of the Home Counties was a normal way of life. I suppose, because of his early start and late homecoming, we boys saw little of him during the week. But I do not remember him as in any sense an absent father. I was always fond of him.

Before he met my mother, Father had fought in the First World War, joining up when he was 18 in 1916. He told us little of those experiences - I guess they were too painful – though I do remember him showing me the medals he had won for engaging in battles at the Front. It was not until I read his memoirs after he had died that I realised the utter horror he and millions of others had experienced, going into action as a tank driver, being subjected to shell-fire, having to run for his life on a couple of occasions, being given up for lost, yet somehow surviving, as so many did not, to come home and pick up the threads of life again. I treasure an album of photographs he took with his little vest-pocket Kodak camera, both during the war and afterwards while he was still serving in Germany. Among these photographs, amazingly enough, are some of the inside of the cock-pit of his tank! Today these would surely have breached the Official Secrets Act! The First World War was ghastly, tragic and inept. It never should have been fought and involved catastrophic loss of life in unimaginable circumstances. As a result of his involvement, while always retaining a deep sense of indebtedness to those among whom he had fought, especially those who had perished around him, my father had become profoundly sceptical about the value of war in any of its forms. I am sure it was a great relief to him and to my mother that, at the age of 41, he was too old to be conscripted for service when the Second World War was declared – though he played his part in fire-watching in the streets where we lived. I have inherited his revulsion at the horrors of war and his longing for peace in the world.

Some of those who later became my ministerial colleagues, particularly those who had no personal memories of the war, found worship on Remembrance Day difficult to handle. For me it has always had an atmosphere, a poignancy and a meaning of all its own and has presented an unique opportunity to lead worship that both honours those who have died in war, including so many of my father's comrades, and also focuses on the Gospel of Peace. I put this down, at least in part, to my father's involvement in World War 1.

My mother was the more dominant of my two parents. Perhaps it was due to her position as the middle child of nine siblings, perhaps to the genetic influence of her father from whom she derived many of her characteristics, but there is no doubt that she exerted the strongest parental influence in our family. What she said, we boys did: not always willingly, but never questioning that we should. If ever we thought to kick over the traces a distinct feeling of guilt would always bring us back into line. She was quite outspoken, taking pride in 'speaking her mind': a good fault in many ways, but not always welcome! She also believed in not giving her children swollen heads: I cannot remember her ever congratulating me on anything I achieved. The nearest she got was when, years after both my brother and I had grown into adults and had learned to drive, she said to me one day 'Tim is a good driver too'! For all that, you knew where you were with my mother and she, together with my father, gave me a rock of truth, faith and love upon which to build my life. At the age of 11 she passed the scholarship and went to Longton High School. I still have somewhere one of her school photographs, taken, as my own school photographs were, on a camera that revolved around the semi-circle in which the students sat. At 16 she gained her School Certificate and thus gained exemption from university matriculation. Her parents, however (like my father's), could not afford for her to continue in school to the age of 18. She therefore left and began to work as what we today would probably call a 'Teacher's Assistant' in an infants' school and, through experience, became what was then known as an 'Uncertificated Teacher'. In those days women teachers who married were obliged to give up teaching, so in 1930 she moved to live with her new husband in Letchworth and did not teach again until my brother and I were in secondary education.

How did a solicitor's clerk from Letchworth in Hertfordshire meet a primary schoolteacher from the Staffordshire Potteries? The Christian Endeavour Movement was responsible. This movement, now I think virtually defunct, was a young people's organisation sponsored mainly by the non-conformist Churches

Keith's Parents' Wedding, July 5th 1930

throughout the country, and indeed across the world, in the early part of the 20th Century. Societies were formed in many local churches, of different denominations, and a regional and national organisation was established. Each year a national Convention was held, which hundreds of young Christians from all over the country used to attend. In 1927 that Convention was held in Nottingham – and the 20-year-old Nancy Goulding and the 29-year-old George Forecast went, met, fell in love, and, after a long-distance courtship, married in 1930. She was 23, he 32. They set up their home in Letchworth, first in a council house, 49 High Avenue, and then in a house of their own: 37 Redhoods Way East. Thus the way was prepared for me to come along in 1935 and my brother Timothy John in 1938.

Letchworth was the first 'Garden City'. My father and his parents had moved there from the East End of London in 1916, possibly seeking solace from the air raids that were beginning to make life difficult for residents in London in the middle of the First World War, and also doubtless hoping for a 'better life' in this spacious new town. They lived in the first council house to be inhabited there - 97 Pixmore Avenue – their first home of their own, having always lived in rooms in London. The town was merely thirty years old when I was born there in 1935. I was named Christopher Keith, my mother having chosen the first name and my father the second. He chose it because it was his mother's maiden name. I have been called by it ever since I first went to school, lest being called 'Christopher' would lead to my being called 'Chris', an abbreviation my mother intensely disliked! I take some pride in the name, partly because of its supposed meaning ('handsome leader'!) but partly also because there is a Scottish clan of that name. It seems that the Keiths were one of the oldest and most illustrious clans, one member being Grand Marichal of Scotland under the famous King David the First in the 13th century. This is the nearest I get to nobility! My grandmother's Grandfather Keith moved from Scotland to London in the early part of the 19th century looking for work, and the family entered the ranks of the working class of East London. There was always a proud streak about my grandmother, however, and also about her brother Arthur whom I also remember, that perhaps derived from their aristocratic background.

I am one of that steadily diminishing number of people who remember life 'before the war'. I suppose most people have idyllic memories of their childhood, and I am no exception. Looking back now, and learning about the history of the 1930s, I realise that all around me was deepening crisis and looming disaster. Economically

Keith and Timothy, 1939

the country was in a slump. Internationally Hitler and his Third Reich were proving to be more and more of a threat to our totally unprepared islands. War and rumours of war were in the air. It was all to explode in 1939. But my memories of that time are all positive, wholesome and pleasant. My life at home was secure, surrounded by love. Specific memories are few but vivid. In particular I remember a holiday at Bognor Regis in 1938 when I was 3. I remember being introduced by our landlady to our bedroom, and to the cot in which she seemed to expect me to sleep, whereas I had been in a big bed at home for at least a year. I remember the sandy beach, and the sandcastles, and the 'boats' my father dug for me. I remember being enthralled by a Punch and Judy Show on the promenade – and how disillusioned I was when I saw the man who operated it pushing it along, upturned, on a handcart, past the window of the room where we were having our evening meal.

My brother Timothy John was born in October 1938. I can remember being taken by my father to visit my mother in the Benslow Nursing Home in nearby Hitchin after he was born. In my mind's eye I can still see the room, and the bed, and the little cot at the foot of the bed in which he was lying asleep. He and I are not alike, either to look at or in temperament. I was always dark, while he was fair, his hair ginger when he was a child. Our voices, however, have always been very similar, both of us having a slight lisp. In her old age even our mother could never tell which one of us was on the other end of the phone! Tim has two sons, Simon and Andrew, and with his wife Janet lives near Halstead in Essex. His lifelong profession was as an architect. Circumstances have meant that we have seen little of each other in recent years, but we make a point of speaking to each other on our respective birthdays.

Much of our family life centred upon the Letchworth Free Church. My father, who had become a member of the Congregational Church in London where he had been brought up, transferred his membership to this interdenominational church when he and his parents moved there in 1916. The church was then only about ten years old and worshipped in a simple building that had been erected by the members with their own hands. By the time of which I am writing, this building had become the church hall and a magnificent building, in a neo-Georgian style, had been put up on a busy street corner at the heart of the town. As I remember it, this modern, light, open building had a large and flourishing congregation. I am told that, when quite young, I liked to count the windows during the service – out loud! At the front was a wide rostrum, with the pulpit in the centre, the organ behind, and a full choir arranged at either side. Below was the communion table, on which sometimes there appeared a large white cloth covering what to me were mysterious objects underneath, which I never even glimpsed. I remember thinking there must be a body under there – which, I suppose, there was in a way, as what I later came to realise were the bread and wine of communion are seen as symbols of the body and blood of Christ.

I think I have always had a tendency to want to change things – at least if an early incident often recounted by my father is anything to go by. At the front of the Free Church there was a car park. Even then, it seems, some people came to church by car! It was customary for drivers to park their cars each side of the entrance, nose in to the grass verge, echelon style. When I was no more that two years old it is said that I asked my father why this was so. 'If I were the minister of this church I'd tell everyone to park down the middle'!

Letchworth Free Church set out to cater for the needs of all Christians, irrespective of denomination – a bold aim in those days. Though there were Anglican churches in three old village parishes nearby, there were as yet only daughter churches in the town itself. Nor were there separate Methodist, Presbyterian, Baptist or Congregational churches in the beginning. Our congregation thus included people from a wide variety of denominational backgrounds. Though the Anglicans did not build in the town centre until the 1950s, the Methodists and Baptists formed their own churches in the 20s and 30s, and thus the high ideals behind the formation of the Free Church were compromised. Perhaps the pioneers were before their time, but looking back it is sad that their ecumenical vision was not more widely grasped.

On Sunday mornings after I turned about three years of age I attended church with my mother (father stayed at home to look after my baby brother) and left after what was then always (and now still often is) called the 'Children's Address'. Father would pick me up and take me for a walk, with Timothy in the pram, until it was time to return to meet Mother at the end of the service. In the afternoons I went to the Sunday School, first in the Primary Department which met across the road from the church in a public hall, then in the Juniors, who met in the church hall. I recall the names of a couple of teachers: Miss Betty Ray and Miss Elsie Savage. They seemed ancient at the time, but when I returned to the church in the late 1970s to lead a conference, both were still very much around, so they could not have been much more than 35 when they taught me on Sunday afternoons!

13

One interesting feature of life in that church was what was called 'The Order of the Morning Star'. As members of this 'order' we children were given a set of dated cards at the beginning of each year, each bearing the picture of a star. We were expected to put these in a box in the church porch as we arrived for morning service. Presumably they were then counted by some unseen hand and a record of our attendance kept. I imagine that those who attended most regularly received some kind of prize at the end of the year. In such ways, now seeming rather quaint, we were encouraged as children to make church-going a habit.

These pre-war days, as I look back on them now, present a picture of a church life that was strong and influential. Many of the leaders in business and community life were among the elders and members of our congregation. People of all ages were there, in large numbers. I remember being proud of the church to which I belonged. In my eyes it was without doubt the 'best' church in the town. It certainly had the most prominent geographical position, as it still has. Sadly, the membership of that church, which was 526 in those pre-war days, has now shrunk to 60 and the number of children has diminished from 242 to 23. Such is the measure of the decline of the Church, not only in Letchworth but also throughout the land, not only in numbers but also in influence. I am glad, however, that I was born when I was and can remember at least some features of the Church in its heyday.

Though I was taken to church from my earliest years, I was not baptised as a baby. The minister in 1935 was a Baptist, the Revd Guy Ramsay, who, naturally, believed that Baptism must be reserved until a person became a believer and could make his or her own profession of faith. I am told that Mr Ramsay suggested to my parents that a retired Congregational Minister within the congregation might be asked to conduct a baptismal ceremony, but my parents were adamant that, as Mr Ramsay was the minister of the church, he should preside. I was therefore 'dedicated' after the manner of the Baptist denomination and was baptised much later, when I became a church member. I cannot remember when I first became a Christian disciple: I think I have been one ever since I was born; and the fact that I have I attribute unquestionably to the parents who brought me into the world and surrounded me with their love and their prayers, and to the church where my earliest years were spent.

On September 3 1939 I went to church, as usual, with my mother, leaving my father at home with my young brother. I can still recall seeing one of the elders of the church emerging from the vestry during the early part of the service and passing a note to the minister in the pulpit. We were not long left in suspense: the news was that Britain was now officially at war with Germany. My mother took me straight home when we came out of church at the usual halfway point, and I vividly remember my parents' distress at the news. I had never seen them so sad, and was never to see them so sad again. The precise cause of their concern eluded me, but I knew it was something bad. I remember curling up in an armchair in the dining room, rejecting lunch and refusing to go with my father to Sunday School that afternoon. My young mind must have realised that life would never be the same again.

Chapter 2
THE WORLD AT WAR – 1935-45

The coming of war changed everything for everybody. Our own family life was not unaffected. Early on we were issued with gas-masks. My brother, who was then only 12 months old, was given a 'mickey-mouse' version: red, with separate eyeholes. I, being older, was the proud owner of an adult model: black, with a wide single window through which to look. We all hated wearing them. Fortunately we never had to do so. They were hot and stifling, and made a noise round the edges when we breathed. Had they been needed that would have been the least of our worries. I had no idea, of course, how deadly was the gas from which they were supposed to protect us. We kept them in purpose-made cardboard boxes with a string that enabled us to carry them round our necks. At the distribution centre in the town where these ugly masks were issued I remember seeing a demonstration of a large mask designed for young babies, complete with baby inside, his feet sticking out of the bottom, crying his eyes out.

At about the same time we were issued with ration-books for food and clothing. These were to be a feature of our life until 1954, nine years after the war ended. At the time it was no big deal for us children: it was simply the way we had to live. I now realise that we who were brought up during the war were the healthiest generation of children the country has ever known, for our rationed diet was carefully balanced. Some of the ingredients of this diet come to mind out of the recesses of my memory still: dried egg in waxed packets from America (complete with stars-and-stripes on the outside), spam, dried bananas – and orange juice in bottles from the clinic.

We were also issued with identity cards: not the costly, complicated affairs with which we are threatened now, but simple folded cards containing our name, address and registration number. My number was DELB 99/2. Had my parents both been at home when we registered, I would have been 99/3, but my father's firm had been evacuated (for a short time, as it turned out) from London to Egham in Surrey, so he registered there and thus I became number 2 in the family.

Not long after the war started I went to school for the first time. I cannot remember whether it was after Christmas 1939 or after Easter 1940, but I do know that I went before I was 5. Where we lived in the town there was no school nearby – one was planned but the war interfered with its building, as it interfered with many other projects. I was therefore sent to a school some distance from the house: Norton Road Infants School. My first teacher was Miss Coppleston: a strict disciplinarian of the old school. I did not take to her, but I think I settled to the work without much difficulty. I had the advantage of having been taught the rudiments of reading by my mother before I went to school. On account of the distance from home, I stayed at school for dinner. School dinners were an innovation at the beginning of the war, offered because some mothers, who had previously stayed at home during the day, began to go out to work for the 'war effort', and were thus unable to provide mid-day meals for their families. They have remained a permanent feature of school life, just as working mothers have. I didn't like school dinners at all! So much so that, because my mother was not one of those who went out to work, I started to walk home for dinner. This entailed a walk of a mile or two through a large area of public open space called Norton Common. I remember dawdling on one occasion, and arriving home rather late, to my mother's consternation and my well-deserved punishment! But would parents these days allow a five-year-old child to walk home alone from school at lunchtime, through a large public common, and then back again in the afternoon? I think not.

Soon I moved from Miss Coppleston's class to Miss Binn's. Needless to say, we christened her 'dustbin'! She seemed very old to us children, and certainly had grey hair secured in a bun in the nape of her neck. I remember nothing of her lessons, but I do remember being chosen to be a pageboy to attend upon the school 'May Queen' in the May Day celebrations that took place. I had a green hat with a feather, and a green cape to wear over my white shirt. As I proudly held the May Queen's train, and we walked out on to the school field for the ceremony, I was looking around to spot my mother among the watching parents and inadvertently tripped over the train. I can still see the May Queen's angry face, and hear her comments, as she turned round to reprimand me!

Before I left the Infants' department my parents transferred me from Norton Road School to the Westbury School, in the opposite direction from home. I think this might have been, not because my parents were unhappy with the teaching at

Norton Road but because Westbury was marginally nearer, and there were other children in the road who went there, so I could walk back and fore with them. Maybe it was also because the journey to the new school did not entail a walk across Norton Common! Mrs Alderman was now my teacher, someone to whom I instinctively warmed, and I settled well in her class. Hazy memories of friends suggest that I got on better with the girls than I did with the boys! Ann Alderman (no relation to the teacher) and Sonia Hutchinson are names and faces that come to mind. At the age of seven I moved into the Junior School and into Miss Dear's class. I responded well to her teaching too, as I recall, and, as a bonus, was delighted when on one occasion I went with my father to a Methodist Church in the nearby village of Stotfold where he was to lead the worship, and discovered that Miss Dear sang in the choir and I was asked to sit with her during the service.

Living in leafy Hertfordshire, we were largely protected from the worst effects of the war. We children were not evacuated; rather we received evacuees into our homes from London. A boy called Brian Mitchell came to live with us for a time and attended the Letchworth Grammar School. We did have an air-raid shelter in the garden, shared with our neighbours, the Lockyers. I can remember only one or two occasions when the dreaded sirens went and we took ourselves off to the shelter. We experienced no bombing, though we heard of the devastation being wrought on London. One incident I remember was when we were walking home from school one day and suddenly a German plane, displaying the dreaded German insignia, flew low over the road. I never got to know why it was there, long after the 'all-clear' siren had sounded. It was said that the pilot had lost his way.

One day during the war, probably in 1942, my father took me to visit London for the first time. We travelled up on what was then called the 'Workmans Train' – cheap tickets in the early morning. I can still remember the excitement I felt as I entered the big city. We visited St Paul's Cathedral and its whispering gallery, Westminster, Buckingham Palace, Downing Street and the Tower of London, though I think we were unable to enter the latter as, being a fortress, it was being used for war purposes. How I enjoyed travelling on the Underground trains for the first time! The buses, I remember, were all painted grey, presumably because it was felt that red buses would in some way attract enemy attention – quaint notion! I have, of course, been to London scores of times since then, and indeed lived there for sixteen years, but whenever I go there nowadays, as I get out of the train, I can still feel the thrill of that first visit.

Christmas, then as now, was a high point of the year for all families. The house was usually decorated, often with paper chains we had made from strips of coloured paper produced for the purpose. We always had a Christmas tree decorated with fairy lights. I recall what seemed like long hours during which my father would unpack the lights from the previous Christmas, lay them out, and test them. Usually they worked in the end! Occasionally, however, our tree was lit with real candles standing in clips that were fixed to the branches: not to be recommended from a health and safety point of view! Christmas dinner would include a chicken – then a rare delicacy – and mother would always have made a lovely iced cake, and a pudding of which we boys always had a lucky stir before it was boiled in the copper in the kitchen. Our presents from Santa came in father's long knee-length socks which he wore only with his shorts on holiday. Usually there would be one larger present each on the floor beneath the sock. Looking back, I wonder how my parents managed to buy the extra food we ate, discover the presents we enjoyed, or find the money to pay for them in those days of austerity – but we were never disappointed.

After a number of years my parents became weary of my father working in London and never knowing when and if the day-time air raids would intrude on his work and travelling. He secured a job in a solicitor's office in Cambridge and in July 1943 we moved there, living in a rented house: 45 Hinton Avenue. Looking back, I guess this was in many ways a wrench for my parents. They were leaving the town in which they had started their married life, the house they had struggled to buy, and their friends in church and community. To us lads it was merely an adventure! Cambridge became home, and, if I now look upon anywhere on earth as 'home', then it is to Cambridge that I look.

A feature of war-time life was the 'British Restaurant'. These were established in most communities at a time when the more traditional eating houses were unable to function because of the rationing of food. One of these was set up in a church hall near to where we lived. On the day we moved into our new house we went there for lunch. I am unsure whether we ever went there again, but I can still vividly recall the smell emanating from the kitchen of food being cooked – a smell similar to the one I already associated with school dinners. It is not a happy memory!

My brother and I went to the Morley Memorial School, just around the corner from where we now lived, and opposite the aforementioned church hall. The head teacher there was Miss Kay Murgatroyd, whose nature seemed to reflect her stern-sounding name: a martinet of the old school, whom we respected and instinctively obeyed. My class teacher at the beginning was Miss Quinney, who had come out of retirement at the beginning of the war to return to teaching when others were conscripted to serve in the armed forces or other directed war work. She seemed ancient to us children! Another martinet, it would seem that she must have had experience in the Girl Guide movement, where it was (and perhaps still is) the custom for the leader to raise one hand in the air when requiring silence. Miss Quinney employed this method, instead of blowing a whistle like the other teachers, to gain our attention in the playground. More than once or twice, when she was on duty, my friends and I would miss the signal and be left shouting at each other in the corner, quite oblivious of the fact that all the other children had seen the signal and had gone quiet and still! After a year in the next class, under the care of Miss Auld who was much younger than Miss Quinney, and whom we all liked, I spent two years in the 'top class' where Miss Gray was my teacher. I remember her with great affection. She was an excellent teacher: formal, but fair, and she communicated her enthusiasm for every subject she taught us. As with the Sunday School teachers at Letchworth, however, I thought at the time that she was very old, only to discover in 1996 that she was still alive in Cambridge, now 86. So she must have been only in her 30s when I was in her class!

My great friend during these years was David Yarrow. He and his family had arrived in Cambridge from Lincoln not long before we did and Miss Quinney instructed me to sit next to him in her class. We became firm friends and remained so throughout Junior and Senior Schools, on into University and for many years of adult life. David played the organ at our wedding, but moved to Canada in the 1960s – first to teach, then to become an Anglican priest. We kept in touch and met when he and his wife Pamela came 'home' with their young daughter Alexandra to visit his parents. When we had medical examinations in preparation for entering the Royal Air Force it was discovered that David had a leaking heart valve. These were the days before open-heart surgery was available, and David was judged unfit to serve. Sadly, in the mid 1980s, he died of a heart attack. I remember him with great affection.

As before in Letchworth, our family life revolved around the local church. Round the corner from where we lived was Cherryhinton Road Free Church – not an interdenominational church like the one we had left, but a Congregational Church in all but name. It was natural for us to attend. Quite soon we got involved. My father became Superintendent of the Sunday School and I was invited to join the choir which was led by Mrs Pay, the wife of the minister, the Revd Sidney Pay. But Cherryhinton Road was not Letchworth Free Church! It was struggling under a rather uninspiring minister whose wife had a somewhat dominant and awkward personality. After a while a convenient escape opened before us. In 1944 my father, who had been a lay preacher since his early twenties, was invited by the Moderator of the Eastern Province to become lay pastor of the small village church in Fulbourn, three miles away. He and my mother began to cycle there for morning and evening services on Sundays but decided to make other arrangements for us boys. A few doors along the road lived Mr Herbert and Mrs Mildred Drake — lovely people, who were members of Emmanuel Congregational Church in the centre of the town. That church had a Children's Church, so called, that met at the same time as morning worship. So it was arranged for us to cycle there with Mr and Mrs Drake, which we did until we were old enough to go on our own. Thus it was that we entered the vibrant and stimulating life of Emmanuel Church, for whose influence and nurture I shall never cease to be grateful. We also developed a limited involvement in the church at Fulbourn, attending there on light summer evenings with our parents. This was a very different situation from the one which was becoming our experience at Emmanuel. In those days Fulbourn was a typical East Anglian village: rural, unsophisticated, still to some extent feudal in its atmosphere, presided over by the 'Lord of the Manor', whereas Cambridge was, as it still is, a unique university town (not then yet a city) with a rich mingling of town and gown. Fulbourn Congregational Church reflected the sociology of the community, consisting principally of farmers, labourers and artisans. It had never been a large church, but at the time of my father's arrival it was at a low ebb with only 24 members. The Church Secretary was Mr Francis Chaplin, something of a village personality, who was already 93 years old: quite a significant age then. Nothing happened of which Mr Chaplin did not approve, but that meant that very little happened! Thus I experienced, early in my life, a small village church as well as a large town church: experience that has been of inestimable value as my own ministry has developed.

I have a couple of pleasant memories of the Fulbourn chapel. One is of the Harvest Festival services that took place there. These were days long before socially-minded congregations started the practice of having a mere token display of harvest produce on such occasions, giving money instead of fruit and vegetables to a worthy cause. Fulbourn chapel was decked out with a lavish display: sheaves of corn straight from the fields, piles of the produce of people's gardens, apples and pears tucked between the pipes of the organ, grapes hanging from the pulpit-fall, flowers everywhere, and a large marrow competing for attention at the centre of the communion table with the specially baked harvest loaf. Still today, when I attend or lead a Harvest Festival service and sing the traditional harvest hymns, my mind goes back to those occasions; I can even smell the characteristic harvest smell in my nostrils! On the Monday evening, following the special Sunday services, there would be a further service with a visiting preacher, after which the produce would be auctioned for a particular good cause.

The other pleasant memory concerns the organ. Like many church organs in those days it was powered, not by electricity, but by a hand pump at the side. On occasion my brother and I would be enlisted to operate this device. If we wanted to be particularly mischievous it was possible to let the air out gradually towards the end of a hymn or voluntary so that the music came to an unexpected and squeaky end, to the annoyance of the organist and the subdued mirth of some of the congregation!

During the time my father was giving lay ministry at Fulbourn he was encouraged to study for ministerial recognition. He had always had yearnings in that direction – indeed, he had once cherished the possibility of becoming a foreign missionary – but had been prevented by his lack of formal education. There was in those days in the Congregational Union a strange category of ministry rather inelegantly called 'List B'. Those in this category were originally seen as evangelists, working without stipend in communities to bridge the gap between the Church and those beyond its influence. They were not ordained but were given the courtesy title of 'Reverend'. Gradually, in the days when each local congregation was responsible for paying its own minister, these 'List B' ministers began to be called to the pastoral charge of small congregations which could not afford stipendiary ministry. Mostly they continued in secular employment, though more and more of them came to be paid – at a lower level than ordained ministers. To all intents and purposes they were ministers, but in a totally anomalous position. Sometimes, understandably, they were seen by some both in the churches and among their own number as second class ministers. Eventually the situation was seen to be intolerable, the list was closed, and those who wished it were ordained. But in 1945 there was still a 'List B' and it was possible to access it through home study and examination rather than by full-time college training. It was this opportunity that was offered to my father, and he took it. How he managed to deal with the study in addition to his daily work and his regular ministry at Fulbourn, leading worship twice every Sunday, I shall never know. He must have had wonderful support from my mother. But in 1946 he passed the examinations and was admitted to the Roll. He remained a non-stipendiary, spare-time minister for a good many years but a lifetime calling had been fulfilled. In 1960, the year I was ordained, he and my mother moved to Sunningdale in Berkshire where he took up a stipendiary post and then in 1964 they moved to Ipswich where he became minister of the Crown Street Church. He underwent further training, in 1965 was admitted to 'List A', and was finally ordained at the age of 67. He was encouraged to see this ordination as much as a recognition of all the ministry he had previously conducted, and a seal on that, as it was authorisation for the future. Mother and Father remained in Ipswich after he retired in 1969. He guided the Crown Street Church to unite with the nearby Tacket Street Church and was appointed as honorary assistant minister there. For a number of years, until he was past 80, he continued to lead worship in various churches and acted as Free Church Chaplain at the local hospital. My father has always been an inspiration to me.

During the war seaside holidays in this country were impossible. The coast was ringed with steel and the beaches were mined. Somewhat bizarrely, our family holidays during this time were often taken with my grandparents in the Potteries. From pleasant Hertfordshire, and later Cambridge, we travelled to grimy Stoke-on-Trent – and we boys loved it! It was a different world for us. The grandparents lived on a hill overlooking the town with its industries. The view from the dining room window included, to the left, the Florence Colliery, with its enormous slag heap and little railway along the top carrying the waste material from the mine to be dumped, and, to the right, the innumerable bottle-shaped chimneys of the pottery factories, all belching forth acrid smoke all day long. A greater contrast from our home would be harder to imagine. But I think it was visits like these that gave me an understanding of northern industrial life that stood me in good stead when, decades later, I moved to Manchester to minister in a similar context. I have never felt a stranger in the north.

These visits also gave me a taste of Methodism. My own church life was increasingly Congregational, nurtured by a father who was deeply committed to the Congregational way. There were times when I was close to believing that

Congregationalism was written into the New Testament! But my mother's family were all Methodists – 'staunch Methodists' as they are often described. The Potteries were the seed-bed of Primitive Methodism, whose origins were traced to a 19th century evangelistic movement centred on nearby Mow Cop. My maternal grandparents, however, had been reared in what was then called the United Methodist Church – an amalgamation of at least three former strands of Methodism. In 1932 these different denominations had united with the Wesleyan Methodists to become the Methodist Church, but the old loyalties remained ten or more years later – as, in some places, they still do to this day. My mother's family were steeped in these traditions, and I was to absorb a good deal of the ethos. To this day I am fond of the hymns of Charles Wesley and the tunes of the Methodist hymnbook. I have only to hear 'And can it be' sung to be transported back to the Potteries Methodism of my childhood. In more than three hundred places in Britain the Methodist and United Reformed Churches have come together in Local Ecumenical Partnerships. There are times when United Reformed Church people in these partnerships find the Methodist structures somewhat inflexible and difficult. When I have had experience of these difficulties I have been grateful for my working knowledge of Methodism, derived from my family background.

As I mentioned earlier, living where we did. we were to some extent cushioned from the effects of the war. I do remember, however, the sound of artillery gunfire in the night in the distance after we had moved to Cambridge. And I can still hear, when I think of it, the slow rumble of pilot-less planes, popularly called 'doodlebugs', as they flew slowly overhead, none of us knowing when their fuel would be exhausted, and their engines would cut out, and they would fall to earth with devastating effect. These, and the more threatening V2 rockets that came a little later, were Hitler's last desperate attempt to subjugate Britain.

In May 1945 the war in Europe came to an end and that in the Far East concluded in August. I can still feel the sense of relief felt by the whole nation. Looking back, I don't recall a sense of "we've won" so much as "thank God it's over". We celebrated – how we celebrated! Crowds gathered on Parker's Piece, an open space in the centre of Cambridge, and my father took me to share in the festivities. Whole streets, ours included, arranged parties, closing the road to traffic and setting up tables for eating. Where the food came from, in days of stringent rationing, I never knew, but it was a memorable time. Churches held thanksgiving services on the day that peace was declared. I attended the one my father arranged in Fulbourn, one of the few times in my memory that the chapel was filled with worshippers. I joined the choir as we sang Handel's 'O lovely peace'. I think we must have held a special assembly at school, for I associate with this time my learning of the hymn 'I vow to thee my country' – a hymn which I later came to dislike, with its line which vows to my country 'the love that asks no question.' The victory over Japan was a more muted affair. We all realised that it had been achieved only by the use of atomic bombs in Hiroshima and Nagasaki, with all the devastation they had wrought and the millions they had killed, and there was some foreboding for the future development of such weapons. But we celebrated the victory nonetheless, with fireworks in the garden as I recall. A new era was beginning.

Soon after we moved to Cambridge I began to learn to play the piano. Miss Branch was my somewhat Victorian teacher. I took to the lessons, however, and began to move through the various grade examinations upon which children embark. Later, when I was about 16, I started to learn to play the organ under the tutorship of the organist at our church, Miss Joan Wrycroft. I still enjoy playing for the occasional service, but sometimes wish I had taken the practice more seriously and become more proficient.

Washing day was a weekly event in our family. From my bedroom above the kitchen on Monday mornings (always on Mondays) I could hear my mother, who had risen early, getting the 'copper' going, in which the clothes were to be boiled. When they were ready they were taken from the copper to the mangle, where every drop of surplus water was squeezed out of them. Then, on fine days at least, they were hung out to dry. After that they went through the mangle again – I never quite knew why! – and then were ready for ironing. My mother, in her fastidiousness, ironed almost every item, even the underwear! She was always particularly pleased when she was able to get all her washing cleaned, dried, ironed and placed in the airing cupboard on the same day. Not until I had left home for the RAF did she graduate from the copper to a twin–tub washing machine.

Our first family holiday after the war was spent in Sheringham, on the Norfolk coast. The beach had been mined, and the central part of the pier at nearby Cromer had been demolished, as had happened to the piers as all the resorts round the coast, to hamper any potential invasion. What made the authorities think that invading troops would need the piers on which to land I have never understood! Part of the beach had, however, been cleared of mines and we made the most of it. We stayed in Mrs Cox's boarding house, renting what were then called 'apartments', whereby we bought the food and Mrs Cox cooked it – a suitable procedure in the days of food rationing.

While we were on holiday, the 1945 General Election took place and Labour won its historic landslide victory over Mr Churchill's Conservatives – to my parents' great satisfaction. I thus moved from childhood into youth at a time when the modern Welfare State was being established, with all its benefits to families like ours who, though now middle-class in values and outlook, were not at all well off. Family holidays in subsequent years took us to Sandown in the Isle of Wight, Margate on the Kent coast, and Frinton in Essex. How different such places are from the continental destinations to which members of my family and I now go – but I do not think our holidays were any less enjoyable.

Chapter 3
PEACE AND PROSPERITY – 1946-54

In those days children in their final year at junior school took an examination called 'The Scholarship'. It involved papers in Maths and English and an intelligence test. In Cambridge, those who passed were then expected to attend an interview at the school of their parents' choice. Many children, of course, failed at one or other of these hurdles. Somehow, however, I was unaware of them! My parents had indicated that they would like me to go to the Perse School if I passed – which I did. My friend David Yarrow came with me, though when we arrived we were placed in different forms: he in 1A, I in 1Alpha. The Perse School had begun life in 1615 as a Public School. Formed for the education of 'the public' it had, like so many of its kind, become a somewhat exclusive institution for people who could afford the fees. It had been unable, however, to maintain its independent status and, under the 1947 education act, it had become a 'direct grant school', retaining some of its autonomy but, by virtue of its government grant, able to accept entrants who 'passed the scholarship'. It was for boys only: secondary education in those days was rarely co-educational. We were encouraged to be very proud of our school – and we were! Our school uniform consisted of a blazer, a cap and a tie in purple, black and white stripes. We were obliged to wear it, not only to school but whenever we went out into the streets of Cambridge during term time. Thus our pride in our school was fostered. Such stringent rules are no longer tenable, I imagine, in any school today. The casual off-duty 'uniform' of blue jeans and tee-shirts is more likely to be the order of the day.

The school was then situated near the centre of the town, opposite the massive neo-Gothic Roman Catholic Church. The church clock had a unique chime, which sounded every quarter of an hour. I can still hear that chime in my mind to this day. The school moved to a new building on its playing fields in Hills Road after my time, and the premises there have been expanded several times since that move.

In form 1Alpha the form-master was Mr Ramsbottom, though of course, as is the custom in secondary schools, we had different teachers, in different rooms, for each subject. I enjoyed Mr Ramsbottom's teaching of Geography and treasure his remark on my first school report: 'A pleasant personality, a pleasure to work with'! In school we were invariably known by our surnames and in class we sat in alphabetical order. Next to me sat Fuller – Graham Fuller, who had come to the school from a primary school at the other end of the town. We became firm friends and kept in touch over the years. He and his wife Olwyn lived in busy retirement in Seaford, in Sussex. Sadly, I recently heard news of his death. Though predominantly a day-school, there were two boarding houses situated some distance away from the main building. Unusually, one of these houses (Hillel House) was for Jews, giving me valuable early experience of people following another religion. There were tensions between us – not least because they were boarders and we were day-boys, and because, unlike the rest of us, they did not attend school on Saturday mornings as they had to attend their synagogue. Also, together with the Roman Catholics, they were absolved from attendance at the daily morning assemblies. Looking back, I think that not enough opportunity was taken to explore these tensions and enable constructive discussion between the followers of different faiths. It was not until many years later, when I found myself living amongst Jews in Cardiff, London and Manchester, that I learned as much as I now know about Judaism. At the school, during my time there, the Jewish house was disbanded, presumably because of lack of applicants, and the two boarding houses became Junior and Senior. There were still some Jewish boys in the school, however, and at least one Jewish teacher, Mr Maurice Wollman, who taught us English – and they were still absolved from attendance on Saturdays and from morning assemblies, thus incurring the envy of the rest of us!

Each school day began with an Assembly in the hall. This took the same form every day: a hymn, sung from the Public School Hymnbook, a Bible Reading, a prayer and the Lord's Prayer. Those who were absolved from attendance then came in and notices were given. The whole thing was a little perfunctory. At the beginning of each term the Bible Reading was the first chapter of the Book of Joshua. At the final assembly before the end of each term it was Psalm 121 – appropriately for Cambridge, with its flat terrain, with the opening words: 'I will lift up mine eyes unto the hills'! I can still recite these texts, from the Authorised Version of the Bible.

The school day at the Perse was always a full one. There were five forty-minute periods, with a break, in the morning and three, without a break, on some afternoons. Our masters varied in their approach and effectiveness. Some, I now realise, were right at the beginning of their teaching career, in some cases having recently been demobilised from the Forces. Others were much more senior, having taught there before and during the war. On Tuesday and Thursday afternoons we had sports: a variety of Rugby, Hockey, Athletics, Cricket and Tennis according to the season of the year and, to some extent, personal preference. I was no sportsman, but did play Hockey and Tennis, scored for Cricket and did some athletics, in the different seasons. In the latter I specialised in hurdles. I seem to have been jumping hurdles from time to time throughout my life! On Saturday mornings we had one less period of study and then went for a Christian act of worship at the nearby St Paul's Church, where we heard a variety of preachers. Saturday afternoon was dedicated to sports matches for those who were chosen to play for school teams. I was not chosen!

Curricular activities were supplemented by after-school clubs and other activities including the Scouts and the military Cadet Forces. With our time thus filled to capacity, and when, as in our family, some of us also got involved in church activities, there was little time for or interest in the kind of negative activities and vandalism that are proving to be such a problem among young people in today's society. In my first year at school I took up with the Scouts, but had to relinquish this activity when, in year three, I joined the Cadets – first in the Basic Section and then in the Air Section. In those days, when military conscription loomed over us at the end of our school career, we were encouraged to prepare by belonging to Cadet Forces at school. Looking back, I think it helped to instil a sense of self-discipline, for which I am grateful, but also a sense of patriotism bordering at times on jingoism, which I have since radically questioned. But these were the immediate post-war years, when memories of conflict were still raw and the threat of further warfare was an ever-present reality.

A great bonanza was staged in London in November 1947. Princess Elizabeth married Lieutenant Philip Mountbatten in Westminster Abbey. The country went wild. Post-war austerity and depression were thrown to the winds at least for a day. We had a day off school to celebrate and I went to my friend David's house to listen to the service on the wireless – no television then. Looking back, I am sure that the powers-that-be organised the whole occasion with an eye to giving the nation the lift it needed at that time – and it worked. Now as I write the Queen and Prince Philip, as he became that day, have recently celebrated their diamond wedding – the only reigning sovereign ever to reach this anniversary. The stability of their marriage, still strong even though it has been lived out in the constant glare of the public spotlight, has been and continues to be an example to us all.

One morning at school, when we were all sitting on the hall floor waiting for Assembly to begin, Graham Fuller next to me (we sat alphabetically in the hall as well as in the form room) asked me if I'd like to come with him to Crusaders. He had begun attending this non-denominational Bible Class on the previous Sunday afternoon. I agreed to go. As it happened, it met in Emmanuel Church Hall and was led by Mr Ron Bonny and Mr Harry Fogg. I quickly became immersed in this organisation, attending regularly on Sundays, later playing the piano for the singing of hymns and choruses, attending the weeknight Bible studies (called 'Keenites'), and looking forward to the annual camps held, under canvas, in a variety of seaside places: the Isle of Wight, Studland Bay in Dorset, Polzeath in Cornwall, Sidestrand in Norfolk. The Crusader movement sets out to serve secondary school pupils and to communicate to them an evangelical form of Christianity. As in the schools in those days, boys and girls were segregated. I revelled in its activities and the movement had a great influence upon me, an influence I gladly acknowledge to this day. It provided deep fellowship, opportunities to probe the Christian Faith and its implications, and the development of leadership skills. It also gave me a love for and a working knowledge of the Bible. As a symbol of this I retain, in a place of honour, the Bible (Authorised Version) I was given when I had attended regularly for fifty consecutive Sundays and was admitted to the 'Order of Crusader Knighthood' in July 1948. Paradoxically, I never accepted the conservative, almost literalist interpretation of Scripture upon which the Crusader movement was based. My membership of Emmanuel Church, with its more liberal stance, was a counter-balance to that. But I honour both influences upon my spiritual development. Without the latter I might never have become committed to Christian social and political action, for there was none of that mentioned in Crusaders. Without the former I might never have become committed in a personal way to Christ as Saviour and Lord. Though my own theology has moved away from that of the Crusaders, I shall always be grateful for its influence. I hope I have retained something of its evangelical urgency in my own ministry.

While some of my friends and I were at a Crusader Camp one summer news came through to us that Peter Bonny, the young son of the leader of our Crusader Class, had died of Poliomyelitis. This was a dreaded disease of the central nervous system that frequently caused paralysis of the limbs and sometimes led to the death of the sufferer, as in this case. There was no known cure at the time. Since then an inoculation has been discovered and all parents have been urged to have their children treated, often by drops on a lump of sugar. The result has been that the disease has been virtually eradicated. How much we owe to medical science. Measles, Chickenpox, Mumps, Whooping Cough, Diphtheria, Tuberculosis, Smallpox – diseases that were all prevalent during my childhood and some of which I contracted - are now virtually unknown. Yet much more deadly diseases like Cancer and AIDS have replaced them. We have a long way to travel until the world is free of disease.

A large part of life for some of us at the Perse School was taken up with amateur dramatics. I joined the Perse Players which, in those days, were concerned exclusively with producing the plays of Shakespeare. We were proud that the well-known Shakespearean actor Marius Goring had been a student at the school and had begun his acting career in the Perse Players. I am proud that my first lines on the stage were in the role of Hamlet's servant, when Peter Hall, later to become famous as an actor and producer, was acting the title role. From this humble beginning I went on to act as Theseus in 'A Midsummer Night's Dream', Buckingham in 'Richard III', Mr Page in 'The Merry Wives of Windsor' and Alonso in 'The Tempest'. I have kept copies of the school magazine, 'The Pelican', from the whole of my time at the school, and it is interesting to turn up the reviews of the plays in which I took part: 'CK Forecast played a rather dull part with a light and pleasant touch'; 'CK Forecast invested an unrewarding part with great plausibility'; 'CK Forecast needed more guile, more craft, and indeed the simulation of more years, but he acted with gusto'; 'CK Forecast showed assurance, dignity and control in speech and gesture'. Our producer was the senior history master of the school, Mr John Tanfield – a somewhat idiosyncratic character of whom we became very fond. I can remember hardly any of the lines I learned now – I even had to think hard to remember exactly which parts I had played! - but I thoroughly enjoyed the experience at the time, and am sure it was immensely influential in developing some of the talents that are useful in public ministry.

Looking at the 'Pelican' of July 1954, where my 'Valete' from the school is recorded, I see that I was treasurer of the Perse Players, that I was secretary to the Music Society, and that I was also a member of the school choir. Each term we had a school service in St John's College Chapel at which the choir sang at least one anthem. Just before my voice broke I sang the alto solo 'He shall feed his flock like a shepherd' from 'The Messiah', It was my only venture into solo work! But I enjoyed all choral work – a trait I perhaps inherited from my mother's father - and it is a delight, after many decades without such involvement, now to be singing in the Colwyn Choral Society.

In the street behind the school was the University Cricket Ground, Fenners. Though I had little enthusiasm for participative sport, I enjoyed watching it, and during the summer term frequently popped into Fenners with my friend David at lunch time and after school to catch a glimpse of first-class Cricket, usually quite free. There I watched the likes of Peter May and David Shepherd playing for Cambridge, Dennis Compton, Len Hutton, Cyril Washbrook and other household names in the visiting County sides, and, a rare opportunity, Don Bradman towards the end of his career, playing for the Australian touring side. This was a privileged existence!

While I had been progressing through the school, from year to year, I had been increasingly involved in the life of Emmanuel Church. The minister there from 1946 – 1956 was the Revd John Murray. He had been a young friend of my parents in Letchworth, where he was a reporter on the local paper, 'The Citizen', and a member of the Free Church. My father (and he too) loved to tell the story of how, one evening in 1937, he called on my parents and spent the evening chatting. As he was about to leave, my father asked him, almost out of the blue, whether he had ever thought of applying to enter the Christian ministry. The young man blushed, and confessed that he had called that evening to discuss that very matter, but had not had the courage to broach the subject. From that moment John applied, trained, and entered the ministry, being ordained at Buckhurst Hill in metropolitan Essex in 1942 and coming to Cambridge four years later. Afterwards he served in Bath, Mill Hill in London and Trowbridge. Sadly, he fell victim to Alzheimer's disease and was cared for in a nursing home in Bristol until he died in 2008. He always said that, but for my father's question, he might never have discovered his calling. The same kind of experience came to me much later, and this incident reminds me that I have often said, when seeking to address the need for ministers, that many people who are now in the ministry could tell a similar story; and I have tried to encourage people to identify suitable candidates and put the all-important question to them.

Emmanuel Church was seen then, and perhaps still is, as one of the most influential Churches in the land. It had a large congregation, made up of University dons, academic professors (PhDs were ten a penny!) professional people in influential positions in the town, together with clerks, labourers and college servants. In addition, it then attracted scores of university students. A Society existed for their nurture: The University Congregational Society – 'Cong. Soc.' for short. The worship, led by 'JM' as we knew him, was orderly, straightforward, scholarly and challenging, and many of us who belonged in those days have good reason to be very grateful. The fellowship was dynamic, caring and progressive. I could not have wished for a more stimulating church to which to belong as I grew through my teenage years. When I was 16, having participated in a class for people of my age led by the minister, I requested Baptism and Church Membership.

John and Mary Murray, in their previous Church in Buckhurst Hill, had been near neighbours of the Free Church in Woodford Green in Essex. That church, under the ministry of the Revd Eric Hodgson, had been one of a number selected to experiment with what was then called 'The Family Church' movement. A minister who later became one of my 'idols', the Revd Bert Hamilton, when ministering in Bolton, had had a vision of the Church as a family of people of all ages, to which children and young people belonged equally with the adults. According to his vision, Sunday School on Sunday afternoons was abandoned and children were encouraged to attend morning worship with their parents or with designated 'Church Friends'. They would share with all members in the first fifteen minutes of worship and then move to departments suitable for their own age group. Thus parents and children would be enabled to attend church together, at the same time, rather than children going at a different time to a different place. So they would, it was hoped, grow to spiritual maturity within the church family just as they grew to physical maturity within their natural families. Having successfully developed his vision in Bolton, Bert Hamilton moved to London to become Youth and Education Secretary of the Congregational Union and was able to share the vision more widely. Before long churches of many denominations began to implement it. Today there is hardly a church in the land that continues to hold a Sunday School of the former kind. Coming to Cambridge in 1946, John and Mary Murray, with their experience at Buckhust Hill behind them, set about putting the concept into practice at Emmanuel Church and it was as a young member of this 'Family Church' that I experienced my own spiritual development. I began as a member of the children's groups. Then, at the age of 14, with three or four of my contemporaries, I began to teach a group of children aged 4-6 in the Primary Department.. The leader of that department at first was a dedicated young woman called Mary Robertson, later to be succeeded by my mother. The standards were high. We were expected to attend 'Training Class' weekly to study the following Sunday's theme at our own level and thereafter to prepare for the ensuing session with the children. This kind of regime would be unlikely to be possible today, and in any case the number of children in our congregations has drastically reduced. But it gave me high ideals and a rich early experience which coloured the whole of my ministry, both in the pastorates I served and when I myself moved to a post in central London not dissimilar to the one Bert Hamilton had occupied so many decades earlier.

When I was about 16 I joined what was called the 'Young People's Preaching Group' led by members of the church a little older than myself. It was as a member of this group that I started to lead worship in the village churches around Cambridge, though I had already had some limited experience of this activity at services led by my father at Fulbourn. Looking back, I cannot imagine how effective these services were, but the congregations were very kind and encouraging. When I was about 17, with my father's encouragement, I began to lead worship on my own. My first such service was held in November 1952 in the village of Kingston, some miles to the west of Cambridge. The church there met in a delightful converted thatched cottage and had a lovely atmosphere all of its own. On that particular evening things seemed to be going satisfactorily, when, during the first hymn, the door opened and my parents, aunt and a friend entered, having, unbeknown to me, caught the bus from Cambridge in order to be there. I think I survived this incursion! I could not have had a better start in Christian living than that which was provided by the influences of Emmanuel Church, the little churches in the villages, and my own supportive family.

The one area of my development that was held in abeyance for the time being, I can see now looking back, was close contact with members of the opposite sex. Secondary schools were rigidly segregated. The Perse School for Girls, down the road from our school, might as well have been a hundred miles away for all the contact we had. We did have a joint ballroom dancing class when we were in the sixth form, but in my year the girls' school went down with mumps early in this period and the classes were abandoned. At church I met a few girls of my own age, but there were not many girls in the local congregation, other than the students who were, of course, several years older than I. Our Crusader class, too, was an entirely male world, except for the occasional rather daring meeting between sixth-formers in the boys' and girls' classes, permitted on particular occasions under strict adult supervision. Open, natural relationships had to wait until later.

Everyone in Cambridge rode bicycles, or so it seemed. I understand that many people still do. I had learned to ride, with my father running along behind me, before we left Letchworth, but always had second-hand machines until part way through my time at the Perse School when my parents bought me my first new bike. It cost £15 – a large amount in those days. I was very proud of my new 'Hopper' bike and kept it scrupulously clean. I rode it to school every day, and in the holidays my friend David and I used to ride the country roads around Cambridge, greatly enjoying the open air. Cambridgeshire is flat, except for a range of hills to the south of Cambridge – the Gog Magog hills, supposedly the graves of giants of that name. This presented its own challenges to cyclists – though when, many years later, I returned to the area by car, and travelled up and down those hills in top gear, I realised that their difficulty was purely comparative!

My year at school was the first to be subjected to the new General Certificate of Education, one of the flagship policies of the post-war Labour Government. I sat for the Ordinary Level ('O Level') under the auspices of the Oxford and Cambridge Joint Board in 1951 and passed in English Language, English Literature, Mathematics, General Science, French, and Latin. It will be seen that I was already keen on the Arts, rather than the Sciences. I managed to fail in Greek. A classical language at O Level was a requirement for entrance to Cambridge or Oxford Universities in those days, and, living in Cambridge, it was assumed that we were heading towards a local University career.

In 1951, partly I suspect to engender a sense of positive patriotism into the nation following the deprivations of the war, the Festival of Britain was staged. A large exhibition was set up on the South Bank of the Thames in London, together with a new park at Battersea. We went as a family, and I recall the Skylon, a large mast rather like a totem pole, at the centre of the site, the Dome of Discovery, and the Festival Hall – the latter being the only part of the development which survives. It was all very impressive, though whether it succeeded in its aims I cannot tell. In 2000, fifty years later, an attempt was made to provide a similar focal point to the nation with the creation of the Millennium Dome at Greenwich. It has to be said that this project met with limited success. The London Eye - a great ferris wheel on the South Bank - has been more successful, with its stunning views all over London.

It was in the autumn of 1952, when we were all in our classes, that the whole school received a summons from the headmaster to assemble in the school hall. The sobering news was that the King, George VI, had died. I guess we were all more royalist then than many of us are now, but to a greater or lesser extent we all shared in the nation's grief at the passing of a leader who, with his wife Queen Elizabeth, had been a great inspiration during the war. A few days later my friend David and I, on our way home for lunch, stopped by the railway bridge to watch the royal train pass by carrying the King's body from Sandringham to London. Then we all had a day's holiday on the day of the funeral. Such was the respect given to the passing of a great and good man.

More joyfully, in June 1953 we again had a day off school to celebrate the coronation of Queen Elizabeth II. We had no television in those days, but family friends, the Yateses, had one, constructed at home by the father of that family, Gilbert. It was a large piece of furniture, about four feet high, with a minute screen about nine inches square! But we watched the whole event – history in the making. Memories, apart from the ceremony itself which was most moving, include seeing Queen Salote, the huge queen of Tonga, riding in an open carriage in the pouring rain, greeting the crowds with a wide smile, thoroughly enjoying her moment of glory. Our Queen, in her early twenties on the day of her coronation, is still on the throne over fifty years later. In changing times she has been and remains a symbol of national identity and moral rectitude and manages, by subtle changes in her own style of royalty, to offer a fine example of wholesome Christian living to the nation. Her family, however, have sometimes been a different story. One cannot help wondering where the monarchy will go in coming decades.

The death recently of the iconic climber Sir Edmund Hillary in New Zealand reminds me of the announcement on the morning of the coronation of his pioneering conquest of Mount Everest, in partnership with Sherpa Tensing. It was a fine feat, not to be belittled by the number of those who have reached the summit of the world in succeeding years. Our family interest in the expedition was heightened by the fact that an undergraduate member of our church choir, George Band, was a member of the team.

Easter 1953 saw me attending a conference on the theme of Christian Vocation at Westhill College in Birmingham. This conference was organised by the Revd Leslie Tizard, then minister at Carrs Lane Church in that city and, for that year, Chairman of the Congregational Union of England and Wales. With a concern to challenge young people in the churches to consider their vocation seriously, he had asked certain ministers to nominate individuals who they felt might profit from such a conference. My minister, John Murray, had nominated me. It turned out to be a very significant experience. Sessions were led by people from different walks of life: teaching, industry, commerce, academia – and the ordained ministry. The Chairman, I remember, made it quite clear that he had not intended the conference to be in any sense a 'forcing shop' for the ministry, but it is interesting that quite a number of those present felt the beginnings of a sense of call during that time, myself included, and several entered the ministry as a result. I am immensely grateful to those whose concern and vision initiated that conference and for the influence it had on me at an impressionable age. I have several times suggested that something along the same lines would be worth considering again, but, as far as I know, to no avail.

When I reached the sixth form at the Perse I was appointed to be a prefect. This characteristic of the public school system gives certain students leadership responsibilities within clearly defined limits and, with those responsibilities, a number of privileges. I remember being pleased to receive this appointment, along with a number of my friends. I shudder as I remember the arrogance with which I am sure I carried out the appointed tasks, and the viciousness of the punishments we were entitled to mete out. The cane, in my day, was the preserve only of the headmaster, but the gym slipper was a permitted punishment for prefects to exercise – and we did! Today it would be against the law. The prefects' common room was a pleasant place for relaxation and gossip. I guess the opportunities for leadership development afforded by this experience have had their positive effect upon me as my life has unfolded.

Also when I was in the sixth form a group of us, gathered together by the curate of Holy Trinity Church in the town-centre churches, brought into being the Cambridge Schools Christian Association. Our meetings, held in the Henry Martyn Hall in the town, drew sixth-formers (and I think fifth formers too) from all the secondary schools in good numbers to hear speakers and engage in debate.

This was the age of mass evangelism. Charismatic figures, not usually ordained ministers, with a conservative attitude to the Bible and a passion for conversion, would conduct huge rallies in various cities and had a deep influence on many individuals. This was not a new phenomenon. In my grandparents' time it had been Moody and Sankey from the United States. My parents used to talk of Gypsy Smith here in Britain. While I was at school Tom Rees, a British preacher, conducted campaigns all over the land. He came to Cambridge in 1948 and many of us from our Crusader class responded to our leaders' encouragement to attend. I remember being very impressed by his persuasive personality and oratory, and when towards the end of his address he appealed to people in the audience to make a personal commitment to Christ I found myself responding. Looking back, I do not think that decision was as significant as the evangelist and his team would have considered it to be, but it was a stage on my pilgrimage nevertheless. In 1953 Billy Graham came to Britain for the first time and I attended two of his rallies in Harringay Stadium in London. He was, and still is, a great man by any reckoning. I was very impressed indeed with his preaching and am glad that I had the opportunity to hear him when he was setting out on his ministry. The great contribution of what we sometimes call the 'evangelical' approach to Christianity is that it faces people with the need for personal commitment in a way the more liberal churches often do not. The weakness of that approach, at least in those days if not today, was that it underrated the vital necessity of church membership for Christian disciples and paid scant attention to the need for Christians to get involved in the social and political issues of the world.

Finances were not always easy in our household, my father being involved in a profession that was notorious for meagre pay and my mother not working until we lads were in our teens, and then only part time. We were never made to feel 'poor', however, and, looking back, I honestly cannot say that we felt deprived. Life, of course, was simpler then; teenage expectations were not so high and financial requirements were not so great. As we grew up we were encouraged to earn a little pocket money. Some of my friends undertook morning paper rounds before school, but I did not fancy that. Getting up early and out in all weathers did not attract me! Once I was 16 I used to work for the Post Office every Christmas, delivering the extra mail that accumulates at that time of the year. I continued to do this when, later, I went to university. At that later time I also found work in Boots the Chemists, portering and sometimes serving on one of the counters. I am amused, after all these years, as I recall how one day, when I was serving on the cosmetics counter, an elderly lady was considering the wide range of facial treatments displayed. Evidently thinking I was some kind of expert in such things, she leaned over confidentially and asked: "Excuse me, what would you do with a face like mine?" I hesitated to give her an honest answer! All this was useful experience, and the money certainly helped.

In 1953 I sat, for the first time, the Advanced and Scholarship Levels of the GCE. I gained Scholarship level in English and History and Advanced level in French. On the strength of these passes I was granted a County Major Scholarship and was thus equipped to apply for University entrance, knowing that all the costs of my tuition and living expenses would be covered. How different things were then from what they are today. I suppose only about 12% of the school population moved on to University entrance in those days, and there were far fewer institutions available. State funding could therefore pay University bills and those who were fortunate enough to get there could relax, knowing that, provided they acquitted themselves reasonably academically and were not extravagant in their life-style, they would have no undue worries. Nowadays, many more people have many more opportunities at many more universities, but the obverse side of the coin is that most of them graduate with huge debts that have to be paid off in the following years. In the rarefied world of Cambridge in the 1950s I doubt if any of us in that highly privileged education realised how fortunate we were. I know my parents were deeply moved, as well as pleased, that I could avail myself of opportunities that had been but pipe-dreams for them.

After the age of 18 I stayed on at school for an additional year in the hope of converting my County Major award into a State Scholarship. This would have had two effects: it would have meant more money, and a wooden shield would have been fixed to the wall of the school hall honouring what I had done. In the event I probably spent too long enjoying myself in this final year at school and failed to make the additional grade.

I am very grateful for my 'public school' education. It gave me a fine grounding, not only in the subjects taught and learned but also in the skills needed to live a responsible life in the world. I remember my school days with affection and, inevitably, some nostalgia, and some of the teachers in particular – both those we admired and those we didn't! But I have become ambivalent about selective education. Should not the opportunities it gave people like me be available to every young person in the land? People like me 'succeeded', but what about those who 'failed'? Comprehensive Education was not to come in for another decade or so. I sometimes wonder how I would have fared if it had happened in my time at school. In many places it has fallen on hard times, but at its best it seems to me to offer a broad-based education to all, together with the possibility of preparing many more students than was the case in my day for Higher Education. The Perse School, after I left, moved into modern premises a mile or two away from the city centre and then opted to 'go private'. I think I have more difficulty with that, though I know the school offers generous bursaries to those who wish to avail themselves of its education and cannot afford it. Though ambivalent, I remain grateful for my schooling. As an 'Old Persean' I have not kept in close touch with the school, though I have received the Old Boys literature over the years and recently have subscribed to the school's bursary fund.

Living in Cambridge, and going to school there, meant that we were always very conscious of the ancient university in that town, but only dimly aware of any other. On the wall ahead of us every time we sat in the school hall was a board that contained the names of all those former pupils who had been granted college fellowships. Only two in the whole history of the school had gone to Oxford – the rest had all gone to Cambridge. Around the hall walls were the individual wooden shields referred to above, displaying the names of pupils who had gained college scholarships and exhibitions, together with those who had obtained state scholarships. Almost all had become Cambridge graduates. Living in Cambridge, Oxford was the great 'enemy' so none of us would have considered going there. I doubt if we even knew there were any other universities in the land! Our headmaster allocated us around the Cambridge colleges. He instructed my friend David Yarrow to apply to Jesus. Graham Fuller opted for St Catharine's. I was directed to Downing. In my last year at school I took an entrance examination there and was granted a place to read History. I was the first person in the whole history of my family, on either side, to go to University. I have indeed lived a very privileged life.

Chapter 4
SERVING QUEEN AND COUNTRY – 1954-56

My university career had to be put on hold for two years. National Service was still in full swing in 1954. Unless we had a conscientious objection, in which case some form of non-combatant service was required, we were obliged to enlist in one of the three armed Services. When the time came for me to go I remember being somewhat apprehensive: after all, I was about to emerge from the shelter of home, school and church into an unknown and alien world. But I knew I had to do it, so I faced it calmly and resolutely. My father gathered the family together for prayers on the night before I left home: thus reminding me of the enormity of the step I was about to take, but also reassuring me of the presence that would go with me. I had chosen to enter the Royal Air Force and enrolled at Cardington, in Bedfordshire, on September 15 1954. Helpfully, I met another young man on the train who was going to the same place and we palled up for mutual support. Upon arrival we were required to post our civilian clothes home and were kitted out with basic uniform and other equipment and given our service numbers; mine was 2591577. This number has remained with me for the rest of my life. If ever I need to use a three-figure number for any purpose, like the numerical lock on my brief case, I still use my 'last 3' – 577! I had thus left home and was committed to an unknown future.

It was required of us recruits that we indicated our religion. In those days, when most of the population were nominally Christian, this meant saying whether we were 'RC', 'CofE' or 'PMUB' – that is Presbyterian, Methodist and United Board. The United Board was jointly sponsored by the Congregationalists and the Baptists. All this was a bit of a mouthful to most of those in authority, and we PMUB people were usually relegated by the NCOs to 'The ODs' (that is, Other Denominations) or, more frequently, 'Odds and Sods'.

As good fortune would have it, I discovered that two men in my billet were, believe it or not, Congregationalists: Keith Johnson from Beccles in Suffolk and Howard Jones from Aberaeron in Cardiganshire. There was also the son of a Methodist minister, Robert Franklin. We became friends for the remainder of our time in Cardington and then on into basic training. I also met a lad called Barry Jackson from Barnsley in Yorkshire. He was a practising Anglican but, what was more significant, he, like me, had a place waiting for him at Downing College in Cambridge – to read History! I felt, and still feel, that I was leading a protected life. What could have been a lonely existence thus became bearable.

September is harvest season, and when, following my first 'padre's hour', I attended the station church I found that it was Harvest Festival that day – and they needed an organist! I offered to play. I had nailed my colours to the mast and established my Christian credentials.

After ten days at Cardington we were sent to embark on Basic Training: 'Square Bashing' as it was familiarly known. My friends and I went to Hednesford in Staffordshire. The next eight weeks are a bit of a blur in my memory. Life was designed to be hard, and it was! Discipline was the order of the day. Military training was high on the agenda. Much parade-ground drill filled a good deal of the time. Fastidious cleanliness and tidiness in the billets was required. Seemingly ridiculous orders were to cut grass with scissors and paint the coal in our rooms white. We were under the 'command' of our platoon corporal for much of the time. These corporals were full of a sense of their own importance and ruled us with an iron rod. Looking back, I wonder why we were so frightened of them – they were, after all, only a year or two older than we were! Food in the mess was mediocre to put it mildly, but we ate it, for we were ravenous. Popular understanding was that the tea was laced with bromide, to reduce our sexual urges. Church on Sundays and Bible Study Group during the week were a welcome respite! At first we were not allowed off camp, but five weeks after we went to Hednesford we were given a 48-hour pass to go home for the weekend, and thereafter we were allowed off camp in the evenings and at weekends for short periods. I remember visiting Birmingham city centre on a Saturday, attending St Martin's-in-the-Bullring Church of England on a Sunday morning and Carrs Lane Congregational Church on a Sunday evening, and worshipping with the Congregationalists in Rugeley a couple of times under the ministry of the Revd Alan Lyde, who was partially sighted. The minister at Carrs Lane then was a boyhood hero of mine: the Revd Leslie Tizard. It was he who had convened the conference on the subject of 'Vocation' at Westhill College to which I referred in the previous chapter and which proved so formative for me. He was a fine preacher, but sadly died of cancer in his fifties. The vicar of St Martin's was the

Revd Brian Green, also a preacher of note. Both had a significant influence upon me as I grew up. Do young Christians these days have ministers of this calibre to whom they may look for inspiration and challenge?

After passing out from Hednesford School of Recruit Training some of us who had been accepted for Officer training were sent to the Officer Cadet Training Unit (OCTU) at Jurby, near Ramsey in the Isle of Man. Now we could wear civilian clothes when off duty, provided that, as officer cadets, we always wore a trilby hat! The night before we 'entrained' for Liverpool, to catch the ferry, some of us were in the little railway station at Brindley Heath, just down 'kitbag hill' from Hednesford camp – perhaps to obtain our train tickets, I do not know. A delightful woman in the station office, enquiring where we were going the following day, warned us that the sea was likely to be rough: "My son has been all over the world in ships," she said, 'and he always reckons that the Irish Sea is the roughest in the world apart from the Australian Bight": a good way of quelling our trepidation in the face of the next unknown move! In the event, however, the sea was like a mill-pond, and we arrived in this strange land that is a nation all of its own within the British Isles.

The journey from Douglas quay to Ramsey was lightened for us by travelling on the local narrow-gauge railway – a fascination for me, who had always had an interest in railways, and a source of amusement for all of us who were used to the (then) steam railways of England. The Isle of Man proved to be a fascinating place and I explored its quaint delights whenever I could.

It was now almost Christmas and we were allowed a few days home leave. Imagine our chagrin when we arrived in Douglas to catch the boat, only to find that the sea was so rough the boats could not sail. Cooling our heels around Douglas a friend and I sought out the Congregational Minister, the Revd Ian Sharpe, who, with his wife Moira, entertained us for the evening. We visited them subsequently a few times. At midnight, however, the sea had calmed, gratefully we embarked and our boat sailed.

Officer Training was not unlike square-bashing, except that it was, superficially at least, more genteel. The Warrant Officers in charge of our platoons always prefaced their commands on parade with the word 'gentlemen' – not that they treated us like gentlemen most of the time! The training was rigorous, and included camping under canvass for a week at the Point of Ayre in the north of the island. By now it was winter, and we had to shovel the snow away from the sandbag emplacements before we could pitch the tents! Snow rarely falls in the Isle of Man, but it did that year – and it stayed!

At Jurby I met another Keith: Keith Hawkins, a member of the Presbyterian Church of Wales and a candidate for the ministry of that Church. Together we attended the Presbyterian Church in Ramsey under the ministry of the Revd Ray Sawers. We were warmly welcomed in that congregation and both of us led worship there at different times. 35 years later, when visiting the island as Moderator of the General Assembly of the United Reformed Church, Frances and I visited the church, now a congregation of the United Reformed Church, and it was good to meet again a few members who had belonged there in the fifties. My path and that of Keith Hawkins have not crossed for many years, but it has been pleasant to have news of him from time to time. He concluded his ministry in a church in Cardiff that is very near where we used to live in the seventies, and now I occasionally preach at the Presbyterian Church in Prestatyn, in North Wales, which was his first pastorate. I think we were a great support to one another during our time in the Isle of Man.

The matron of Ramsey Cottage Hospital was a keen Christian and invited us cadets to her home on Saturday evenings. I really appreciated this and tried, after ordination, to offer similar hospitality to young people away from home.

After three months at Jurby I failed to make the grade but was offered what was referred to as a 're-tread'. Not wishing to admit failure, I took the opportunity, and went through the whole course again. This time I passed and my parents came over for the passing-out parade in June 1955.

Now it was time for specialist training. I opted for Fighter Control and was posted to Middle Wallop in Hampshire for two months in the summer of 1955, which turned out to be one of the hottest summers on record. Towards the end of our time there we anxiously awaited news of our postings. We had been asked to indicate where we might like to go: a rare opportunity in the RAF. I put myself down for the Far East, thinking it would be good to see the world at the RAF's expense. I was sent to Norfolk – the Far East of England – seemingly an example of RAF humour! I went as a newly commissioned Pilot Officer to Neatishead, a radar station near the coast, the staff of which lived at RAF Coltishall a few miles away, close to the famous Broads.

Pilot Officer Forecast 1956

Fighter controllers in those days, and perhaps still today for all I know, sat in cabins underground, set out around a large map of the country displayed on the central 'floor', gazing at radar screens. Each cabin had its 'crew' consisting of an officer, a corporal, and a number of airmen or airwomen. The station was staffed around the clock, so we worked in 'watches'. Life was now much more civilised than it had been during training. Hednesford seemed an eternity away. When not on duty we were free to go into Norwich, down to the coast, or, from time to time, home on leave. There was, as always, a station church and Coltishall had a resident chaplain: Padre Elijah Philip Schofield, a Congregational Minister. He and I quickly became colleagues and friends and remained so for the rest of his life. Indeed, I was asked to conduct his funeral in Peny-y-ffordd neat Chester in 2001 when he died at the age of 81. I was able to exercise a preaching ministry from time to time, both at the camp church and in the neighbouring town of North Walsham and in some of the villages. On the camp I organised a church choir. Eli Schofield and his wife Dorothy had open house on Sunday evenings, and many of us from the congregation used to descend upon them for informal fellowship and fun. In this atmosphere good, lasting friendships were made and our Christian faith was strengthened. These were days when large numbers of young people still attended church. Not surprisingly, the average age of the congregation in the station church was low. I doubt if station churches, if they still exist on modern RAF camps, draw anything like so many young, enthusiastic worshippers. But those days were good days, and played their part in deepening my Christian commitment.

It was about this time that my future beyond the end of National Service began to clarify. When I was a boy I often imagined myself becoming an architect, and used to draw plans for houses that one day I might build. But mathematics proved not to be a strong point for me, so architecture was shelved. Interestingly, as I have mentioned before, my brother Timothy, when he left school, took articles with a Cambridge firm of architects, qualified, and remained in that profession for the whole of his working life. Having chosen to read history at Cambridge, I then imagined myself entering the teaching profession. I like to think that both my early aspirations have borne fruit in aspects of the work I eventually undertook. I have always enjoyed opportunities for teaching, and from time to time have found myself involved in building projects in connection with churches where I have ministered.

I think I was always destined for the ministry of the Church. While still at Junior School I used to persuade my brother to 'play at churches' on Sunday afternoons while our parents were sleeping off the effects of my mother's Sunday lunch. In the breakfast room, I would pull the table in front of the door that led to the kitchen, put my child's desk on top and a step-ladder at the back, thus creating a pulpit, and place the tea-trolley below to represent a communion table. Timothy was consigned to 'play the organ' on the washing copper that lived in the corner of the room, and I presided from the pulpit! Was all this a sign of things to come? I think it must have been. Other influences were also, of course, gradually having their effect as I grew up, but, as is so often the case, a catalyst was needed to focus my sense of call. It happened when, not long before I left school, I was attending a conference for young people at Cheshunt College in Cambridge. Sitting one day in the common room, the Revd Cyril Blackman came and sat beside me. Cyril was then the tutor at that college. I remember it as clearly now as if it happened only yesterday. "What are you going to do when you leave school?" he said. "Going into the RAF to do my National Service" I replied. "But what after that?" "Going up to Downing to read history". "And after that?" "Teaching I expect". "Good. But don't forget that we urgently need people in the ministry of the Church and on the Mission Field abroad". That was all, but it was enough. The seed had been sown. And while I was at Coltishall and in the fellowship of the church on that station, I made my decision to seek ordination. Whether it was my upbringing, or my involvement in the church, or a developing experience of leading worship, or the crying need of people searching for meaning all around me, I know not. I suspect it was a mingling of all these influences, plus an assessment of the gifts of personality and ability I had been given, and not least the sustained prayers of my parents and, perhaps, others. But had it not been for Cyril Blackman's conversation I wonder if it would ever have happened. All of which reminds me of John Murray and his conversation with my father. There is a responsibility laid upon members of the Church, sadly not always accepted, to identify people who might be being called by God to enter the Christian ministry.

It was while I was in the RAF that I met Frances Hunt who was, much later, to become my wife. Women were not required to undertake National Service, but Frances had signed on for four years service in what was then called the Women's Royal Air Force (WRAF). Her educational achievement had not been spectacular, partly because of an inability to cope with examinations and partly because her parents had moved her around the country at significant times in her life, not least from Barnsley to High Wycombe in Buckinghamshire just before she was due to sit her GCEs. On leaving school at 16 she worked for a time in a shoe shop in the town where she lived, but decided to 'join up and see the world', according to the advertisements put out by the services at that time. She too was posted to Neatishead and lived at Coltishall, and became a regular worshipper at the station church. She also joined the choir which I led there. I had noticed her from a safe distance for some months and responded positively to her quiet and friendly openness. But it was when she sent me a card for my 21st birthday in June 1956 that I found myself drawn to her more deeply. We spent a good deal of time together during the remaining months of my service. Norwich on Saturdays became the venue for meals out and visits to the cinema. The haystacks in the fields around Coltishall RAF station became favourite places in which to 'rest' on walks around the locality. The doorstep of the NAAFI shop provided a suitable place to 'say goodnight'! We had undoubtedly fallen in love. It was, of course, not 'done' for officers to fraternise with those in the 'ranks' and when our Commanding Officer discovered our developing relationship he threatened me with posting to Tiree! Seeing that I was so near to being demobilised, however, he withdrew the threat. Our courtship, as it was then called, therefore continued, both while I was still at Coltishall and subsequently, fostered not a little by the willingness of Eli and Dorothy Schofield to put their sofa at our disposal! Frances came, like my mother, from a Methodist family. This family had its roots in Leek, not far from the Potteries whence my mother's family came. They do say that men tend to look for wives who resemble their mothers, but those two facts are where the similarity ended in our case! Frances and I were not to marry until 1960 – in those days, candidates for the ministry who were not already married when they entered college were discouraged from marrying until their course was complete. We knew we were in for a long courtship, but by the time I left the RAF we had committed ourselves to one another. We became formally engaged in 1958 when Frances was 21 and I was 23.

I left the service of Queen and Country in September 1956. As I am ambivalent about my secondary school education, so I am about my time in the Royal Air Force. A lot of time and money was spent on my training for comparatively little return. I am sure I did little to influence the security of the nation, but I am equally sure my service, such as it was, did a great deal to influence me. I grew up in those two years. The self-discipline I learned has remained with me. The experience of living and working alongside a wider sample of men and women from the community than I could otherwise ever have encountered first-hand was invaluable. If I were to have my time over again, and thinking as I now do, I doubt if I would have entered a combatant force. My Christian faith has led me more and more to adopt a pacifist position. But I went into the service a somewhat cocooned boy, and emerged a man.

Chapter 5
UP TO UNIVERSITY – 1956-59

October 1956 saw me back in Cambridge and entering the college to which I had gained entrance qualifications two years earlier. Downing College was but a quarter of a mile from the Perse School, so I didn't have far to go! The difference, however, was immense. Most of my matriculation year were, like me, recently demobbed from one of the services. The few who had come straight from school seemed like boys by comparison! But now we were all treated like gentlemen by domestic staff and teachers alike. I had rooms – yes, rooms! – on staircase S in the main court. Having by now responded, if only in my own mind, to what I took to be a call to the ordained ministry, though I had not yet candidated or been accepted, I decided to convert from reading History to reading Theology. My tutor, James Stephenson, was delighted, as I discovered that he taught in the Theological faculty. Downing tended to specialise in Law, History and Medicine, and as a Theological student I found myself in a minority of one. This, however, proved to be beneficial, for it meant I was reading my Theology in the company of men who were reading all sorts of other subjects, and thus had the opportunity to relate my insights to theirs.

In my first term two European crises hit the world. The first was the Suez crisis. President Nasser of Egypt chose to nationalise the Suez Canal, hitherto jointly owned by France and the UK, thus at a stroke gaining control of that vital trade route. The British Prime Minister, Anthony Eden, in partnership with France and with the collusion of Israel, retaliated by invading Egypt 'to protect our national interests', a move that proved to be a huge mistake. Soon after this, in a different part of the world, the Russians took action to suppress a popular rising in Hungary with a ruthlessness that stunned the western world. University students gave vent to their feelings in massive protests in the city. I was sensing the beginnings of the kind of student unrest that was to engulf the continent a few years later.

Despite these crises, the fifties were a time of relative stability for Britain. Food became more plentiful and more varied. In my childhood, chicken was a rare delicacy, put on the table no more than twice a year, one being Christmas. Vegetables were eaten only when they were in season in Britain. Gradually during the fifties, with the advent of factory farming and the development of world trade, these things became staple diet all the year round. There was also more money about for more people and consequently expectations of prosperity became widespread. Prime Minister Macmillan, returning from a diplomatic visit to Africa declared that we had 'never had it so good', and most of us hadn't. The cloud on all our horizons was 'the bomb'. What became know as 'the cold war' between East and West developed and became established and the threat of nuclear annihilation was ever present. The Campaign for Nuclear Disarmament was a vigorous force of protest: its black and white badge became as well known as the Union Jack in the land. I did not join, but had much sympathy with its aims. It was said that to accede to its demands would destabilise the world. The theory was never put to the test.

Entering the University, I returned to Emmanuel Church, where now the Revd Dick Hall had become minister, John Murray having removed to Bath in the early months of 1956. I gladly acknowledge the deep influence these two ministers undoubtedly had on me and on my own ministry, both in style and content. Dick Hall's leadership of worship was, I think, more pastoral in tone than John Murray's had been, though no less profound and relevant. I also joined the University Congregational Society, whose activities I had observed from a distance while I was at school. We met on Sunday evenings in the church hall to be addressed by the great and the good of town, gown and country – another immense privilege. There was also a series of study groups meeting in various rooms on weekday evenings, in which we refined our faith in earnest, and sometimes controversial, discussion. The Society also sponsored a 'preaching group', who met to prepare services around a particular theme and then launched them on one of the many village churches within cycling distance of Cambridge on Sunday evenings, rather in the same way as the Emmanuel Church Young People's Preaching Group, in which I had previously participated, had done. I took a full part in all these activities. In the vacation a team of us students would travel to a church somewhere in England to lead a week or two's 'Mission', visiting the houses around the church and conducting services and meetings in the evenings. I remember visiting Seacombe in the Wirral, Adeyfield in Hemel Hempstead and Tonge Moor in Bolton. Occasionally an ecumenical team, sponsored by the Cambridge branch of the Student Christian Movement, which I also joined, would lead such a 'Mission' in a particular locality. In this connection I have vivid memories of going to Halton in Leeds and working for two weeks with the local Methodist, Congregational and

Anglican churches in that area. The vicar of the parish, the Revd Ernie Southcott, was a memorable and influential figure. In that predominantly working class estate he had had real success with the 'house-church' movement, taking the worship and fellowship of the church into the homes of the people. These were seminal experiences which contributed a great deal to my own spiritual development as well as, hopefully, acting as a catalyst for mission in the congregations we visited. Back at University I eventually found myself on the committee of the 'Cong.Soc.' as we called it, serving for a while as membership secretary, responsible for the oversight and care of around 150 members, most of whom were in church with us on Sunday mornings in term time.

Cambridge must then, if not now, have been one of the most church-going cities in the country. All the churches in the centre of the city, and there were many of all denominations, were full on Sunday mornings. A lot of this activity, though by no means all, focussed on the University. I am sure, however, that the participation of students and teachers did a great deal to enhance the life and faith of the citizens of the town who belonged to these churches and, indeed, maintained them so that we, with them, might enjoy what they offered. On Sunday evenings two major opportunities were available. The University Church, St Mary the Great on the market square, held a series of preaching services at 8.30 pm in term time. There we heard such well-know preachers as Archbishop Michael Ramsay of Canterbury and Dr George McLeod of the Iona Community as well as the colourful and controversial vicar of Great St Mary's, the Revd Mervyn Stockwood, later to become Bishop of Southwark. Down the road at Holy Trinity Church the Cambridge Inter-Collegiate Christian Union (CICCU) held services based on a more conservative theology. All were crowded occasions. The privileges go on and on!

Cambridge in the fifties was agog with ecumenical enthusiasm. My Downing College matriculation photograph, taken in 1956, shows a number of students wearing clerical collars scattered among the majority wearing smart suits and collars and ties. These were young Roman Catholic priests who, following their ordination, had been let loose on the university to gain degrees. In 1956 it was quite unusual for Protestants to rub shoulders with Roman Catholics, such was still the mutual suspicion between us. In Downing College, however, we did mix, though theological conversation tended to be conducted along parallel lines rather than genuine dialogue. Such is a measure of the progress of the ecumenical movement over the past fifty years – progress that sometimes those involved today in trying to move it forward do not always recognise – that friendship, dialogue and partnership are now commonplace. Within the non-Roman Catholic area, however, there was much ecumenical activity going on. Organisations like the SCM fostered it, usually among Christians of a liberal persuasion, and CICCU encouraged it among the more evangelical folk. Our inspiration was Jesus's so-called 'High-Priestly Prayer' as recorded in the Gospel of John Chapter 17, with its telling petition for those who would come to faith as a result of the witness of his disciples: 'May they all be one… that the world may believe.' Many of us seriously believed that there would be a united Church in Britain during our lifetime and we were committed to helping that come about. Sadly, Church unity has moved in different directions over the intervening years.

The method of education in Cambridge then, in every faculty, comprised several elements. For us in the Theological faculty there were morning lectures in the Divinity School, given by professors and lecturers of note. These were supplemented by supervisions, where we had one-to-one weekly sessions with a tutor, reading essays we had written and discussing them. Then, of course, there was our personal reading, which could be as wide-ranging as we liked. None of this was compulsory – a novel experience at first after the obligatory study at school and the regimented procedures of the Air Force! But the desire to achieve kept most of us going. My tutor in Old Testament studies was the Revd Dr Peter Ackroyd, once a Congregational Minister but by now an Anglican priest. My New Testament tutor was the Revd Dr John Robinson, then Dean of Clare College but afterwards to become Bishop of Woolwich and to achieve fame, if not notoriety, a few years later by the publication of a book entitled 'Honest to God'. I revelled in the theological hot-house that was Cambridge in the late 1950s.

Downing College in those days required its students to 'live out' for their second and third years of residence. With my parents living in Cambridge the obvious (and cheapest!) option was to live at home. I am not sure that this worked at all well. By now I had been away from home for three years and had acquired a measure of independence. Now living at home I was expected to revert to the relationship we had had when I was at school, not least giving a detailed account of where I was at any one time and what time I expected to arrive home. I found this restrictive. I therefore applied in my third year to live as a lodger in Cheshunt College, a Congregational theological college. This proved to be a good move, as not only did I thus return to college life and atmosphere but also I was able to attend some of their sessions in sermon construction and pastoralia, which contributed unofficially to my ministerial formation.

It was during my second year at Cambridge University that I decided to formalise my desire to enter the ordained ministry of the Congregational Union of Churches. The system then was haphazard to a degree compared with what applicants these days are expected to undergo. I suppose I had to get the support of my local Church Meeting at Emmanuel, but I cannot remember doing so. I then remember an interview with a few representatives of the County Union of Congregational Churches, followed by an interview at the denomination's central offices in London – the Memorial Hall. My memory of all these stages of the process is, however, distinctly blurred. All I know is that I must have been accepted. Then the decision had to be made as to which college I should go for the further training that was required. I had to make this choice myself and make my own application, I did so by consulting the Congregational Year Book and examining the entrance requirements and the courses offered at the various colleges. I felt it would be unwise to stay in Cambridge, as I could have done, so much of my life having been lived there. The obvious course, people told me, for a person who had graduated in Theology at Cambridge, as I hoped to do, was to go to Mansfield College, Oxford. But, apart from an irrational but perhaps understandable in-built aversion to anything to do with that 'other place', I read that they would require three further years of training and another degree, and I was anxious to get to the point of ordination, not least so that Frances and I could get married! Other colleges in London, Nottingham, Bradford and Manchester also seemed to require a long period of further study, but the Western College in Bristol seemed to offer just what I needed: a further year of practical study to equip me for local ministry. Accordingly I applied and was accepted.

I graduated, with all the pomp and circumstance that typify this unique ceremony in Cambridge, in June 1959. We assembled in gown, wing-collar, white bow, academic bands and hood, in the college main court and paraded to the Senate House, where the proceedings took place in Latin – of course! It was a proud day. I'd been expected to graduate 2/1, but in the event achieved only a 2/2, let down by my inadequacy at Greek and Hebrew. No one, however, has ever subsequently asked me what class of degree I obtained!

Degree Day, Cambridge 1959

Chapter 6
MOVING WEST – 1959-60

Bristol now beckoned. The Western College first arranged for me to undertake what was then called a 'student pastorate' under their oversight at Drybrook in the Forest of Dean – a completely unknown part of the country to me. This took place during the long vacation in the summer of 1959 – a hot dry summer by British standards. I thoroughly enjoyed it. I was to all intents and purposes the minister of the Rehoboth Chapel there for three months. They took me to their hearts and congregations grew. I remember hot Sunday evenings (most churches had two services in those days, and often, as in Drybrook, the evening congregation was the larger of the two) with 60 or 70 people present and a great sense of expectation abroad. I conducted services of Holy Communion regularly (no requirement then to be ordained to do this, or to have District Council permission to do so!) a few baptisms and my first wedding. It is somewhat sobering to realise that that bride and groom will soon celebrate their golden wedding! The culture of the Forest was strange to me. Sandwiched between the Severn and the Avon, close to the Welsh border, it was and is somewhat cut off from the rest of the country, with its own accent, customs and way of life. There was much rural poverty around. In Cambridge one didn't often visit cottages with no running water, no bathroom, and an earth floor in the living room! They had arranged, however, for me to live in rather more sumptuous surroundings – in the home of Mrs Clara Hale and her daughter Daphne, who lived in a fine detached house at Nailbridge at one end of the village. Mrs Hale was a lovely, motherly person and I felt very much at home there. I found the Forest intriguing and it certainly enlarged my experience. One venture I encouraged them to make was to brighten up the inside of the chapel by placing curtains behind the pulpit. I also papered the walls of the vestry in bright yellow and black. The curtains and the wallpaper were still there when I visited thirty years later. I hope I had an equally lasting impact by my leadership of worship and my pastoral care!

My training was, however, not yet complete. In the September of 1959 I took up residence in Bristol. The Western College was non-residential. College life centred on an elegant stone building, since listed, at the top of Cotham Hill not far from the centre of the city, but students had to find their own living accommodation. I searched, and eventually found a basement room with kitchen in a terraced house in Upper Belmont Road, a mile or two from the college. It was a good move, giving me the opportunity of independent living for the first time in my life.

On the day back in 1958 when I had presented myself for interview at the Western College, Howard Starr from Walthamstow in London was also being interviewed. He, like me, was accepted but began his training a year earlier than I. Meeting up with him and his wife, Margaret, when I arrived in 1959, a strong friendship was forged, and when Frances arrived in Bristol following our marriage in 1960 that friendship developed. Over the years we have visited each other's homes on many occasions, and when we found ourselves in the same part of the country following our move to Manchester in 1992 these visits became a regular feature of our lives. They have been wonderful friends, and, now we are all supposed to be retired, we regularly travel the road between their home in the Wirral and mine in Colwyn Bay to visit each other.

In 1959 the college 'house' included about thirty students, all destined for the Congregational Ministry. The college was one of ten recognised by the denomination, all independent foundations, but all training Congregational ministers. The contrast with today, where the United Reformed Church recognises just three colleges for this purpose, and none of them has a house of more than thirty, is marked. It is a sign of the contraction of the main-line Churches in Britain, of all denominations, over the last forty or fifty years.

The Western College week consisted of lectures (shared with the Bristol Baptist College down the road) from Tuesdays to Fridays, conducting worship in the many Congregational Churches around the city and further afield on Sundays, and having a day off on Mondays – presumably to recover from the weekend's preaching! I count it an immense honour that the principal of the college was the Revd Dr Lovell Cocks, then in his final year of teaching before his retirement. 'Doctor', as we called him, was a delight. Theologically astute, he carried his learning lightly, and laced it with a puckish sense of humour. He took pride in telling us that we were the great-grandchildren of the highly influential German systematic theologian, Albrecht Ritschl, who had taught at Gottingen in the 19th century, as Ritschl had taught the Scottish Congregationalist theologian PT Forsyth, and Forsyth had taught Lovell Cocks at New College, London, and Lovell

Cocks was teaching us. I think we were suitably impressed! Lovell Cocks had been Chairman of the Congregational Union in 1950 and had delivered what had been thought to be the most impressive address from that chair in living memory. I have a copy of it still. It is entitled 'A Church Reborn', and reading it today, 57 years after it was delivered, not only can I hear the sonorous tones of the preacher but I marvel at how challenging his words still are, and how little we have heeded what he was saying to the post-war Church he was called upon to lead. A humble man, Dr Cocks was a prophet among us.

The college tutor was the Revd WJ Downes – 'Uncle Billy' to us students. A Congregationalist of the old school, he too was a good and honoured teacher. We never ever saw him without a clerical collar or in anything but a very dark suit! His specialism was comparative religion, though he also taught the Old Testament and Hebrew. Whether or not there was a link I do not know, but he was also a student of Esperanto – that artificial language concocted in 1887 from the roots of many European languages, designed to facilitate international communication. He encouraged us, with little success, to share his enthusiasm!

The weakness of the curriculum I think, looking back, was that it was strong on academic subjects but weak on the practical preparation for ministry. Both our teachers had had pastorates in their early lives, but Lovell Cocks had left his last pastorate in 1932 and WJ Downes had relinquished his in 1947. Their practical experience, therefore, though relevant, was becoming passé, and the world of the 1950s was moving on apace. Pastoralia classes, as they were called, when one or other of them would preside and help us to discuss a variety of pastoral issues, tended to be based on pre-war church experience when life was more settled and secure, and hardly addressed contemporary issues at all. Sometimes I think we students, especially those who were involved in student pastorates, brought more to those sessions than the staff were able to do!

We were taught to preach in what was called 'Sermon Class' – a weekly event that took place in Highbury Chapel across the road from the college. At the appointed hour we would all troop across there and form the congregation while one of our number, taking it in turns, would ascend the pulpit and conduct a service consisting of a couple of hymns, a prayer, a reading – and a sermon. Then we would return to college for lunch, after which we would gather in the Common Room where we would all give our considered comments on what had taken place in the church. At the conclusion of the session Uncle Billy and Doctor, in that order, would deliver their personal verdict, which was never questioned – at least in public! All this was fine, so long as the student whose turn it was on a particular day was reasonably popular in the college community. I recall one occasion when it was the turn of a student who many of us disliked. When he entered the pulpit, all he could see before him were the two members of staff sitting in the front row muffled up in overcoats and scarves. The rest of us were ensconced behind the pillars and in the remote corners of the gallery! Looking back, I can see that Sermon Class had all the potential to become a somewhat cruel process, but we did learn how to preach!

During my year at the Western College, knowing that the principal was about to retire, we students understandably took a keen interest in who would be appointed to succeed him. Eventually the decision was announced: it would be the Revd Basil Sims, then the minister at Redland Park Church, the largest Congregational Church in the city. We were not impressed! Basil had a mixed reception among us, and many of us, while not doubting his ability to be minister of Redland Park, were not at all sure that he had either the stature or the ability to teach others how to be ministers. In our arrogance, we made a formal approach from the House Meeting, asking to meet the Chairman of the Governors to express our disapproval. I guess this was the first example of the 'student protest' that was to become such as feature of university life in the next decade. The Chairman of the Governors, the Revd Kenneth Parry, an elderly retired minister (whom we called 'Drains' on account of his degree being in sanitary engineering!) duly came to meet us, and tried to reprimand us like naughty school-children. Not content with that, he threatened not to grant Leaving Certificates to those of us who were about to leave the college, without which our ordination could not properly take place. Indeed, I can recall a somewhat undignified moment at the final Valedictory Service when Mr Parry was to be seen, kneeling at a chair in the dining room, finally signing these certificates, having left his authorisation to the very last minute. Interestingly, Basil Sims, of course, became principal, but the college gradually reduced in its numbers of students until it was no longer viable and it amalgamated with other colleges in Manchester in 1968 – and Basil Sims, who was initially appointed to the principalship of the united college, withdrew and left the pastoral ministry for secular teaching. Perhaps, in hindsight, the misgivings we students expressed in 1960 were justified by subsequent events.

When, later in 1960, Dr Cocks was preaching at my Ordination service, he remarked that in the summer of 1959 they had wondered what to do with me when I arrived in college for my final year's training, having already got the Cambridge Tripos under my belt. They hit on the idea, it seems, of arranging a supervised student pastorate, and I was introduced to the church at Arley Chapel, not far from the college. Thus, at the beginning of October 1959, I began what would now be called an 'internship' or 'major placement'. The amount of supervision appeared to be minimal – though I am sure the college staff kept their ear to the ground to discern how things were progressing. I thoroughly enjoyed my ministry at Arley during that year, giving me as it did further experience of the work to which I was sure I had been called. In addition, the city of Bristol, which I had not known previously, was proving to be a very pleasant place in which to live – though hillier than Cambridge, and my mode of transport was still a bicycle!

The usual procedure then, when students were ready for ordination, was for them to meet the Moderator of the Province in which the college was situated and to be given an introduction to a pastorate which was seeking a minister. The pastorate would then invite the student to meet the Deacons, conduct services of worship and then be subject to the Call of a Church Meeting. A similar system operated when ministers were seeking to move from one pastorate to another. The system, though now more complicated (not least because the norm now is for Churches to be grouped together in shared pastorates) has not greatly changed. In my case, however, it was different. I duly met the Moderator of the West Midlands, within whose province Bristol was then situated, the Revd Jack Coggan, a somewhat awesome figure. But Arley Chapel, where I was serving as Student Pastor, had already requested the Moderator that they be allowed to call me to be their minister, and he apparently approved of the introduction. It was immensely humbling, after having ministered with these people for several months, to be unanimously called to continue with them into an indeterminate future.

Arley had been a flourishing church before and between the two World Wars, but recently had fallen on somewhat hard times. The fortunes of the district were changing rapidly. Large terraced houses were being converted by unscrupulous landlords into multiple occupancy and housing one of the earliest concentrations in Britain of immigrants from the Caribbean. Those who had once occupied these houses were moving out to the suburbs. All this had contributed to a reduction in the size of the congregation. There had also been a long vacancy in the pastorate.

The membership was then about 70. One member was in her twenties, one or two were in their early thirties, one couple (the church secretary and his wife) were in their forties, but the rest were all over 60 and many over 70. There was, nevertheless, a strong sense of fellowship and commitment, and I had been warmly received and supported during my student pastorate there. It was a challenge, but I was not averse to that. I therefore accepted their Call. So it was that I prepared for Ordination.

Chapter 7
SETTING OUT – 1960-64

My Ordination service took place in Arley Chapel on July 3 1960. The Moderator, the Revd Jack Coggan, presided with great dignity – he was that sort of person. The Revd WJ Downes led a prayer, Dr Lovell Cocks preached what was then called 'the Charge to the Minister' and my minister from Cambridge, the Revd Dick Hall, preached the 'Charge to the Church'. My father led the Ordination Prayer – and performed a similar task at three of my four subsequent Induction services. The Revd John Murray came over from Bath to speak at the reception, which took place in the church hall after the service. It was a high day in the life of the congregation, but also in my own life and pilgrimage, bringing together all the experience that had preceded it and looking forward to what would hopefully be a lifetime's ministry. I can still almost feel the sensation of hands being laid upon my head during that service and the mixture of emotions that went with it: excitement, gratitude, privilege, humility, inadequacy, fulfilment - these are some of them. There have been many and varied experiences since, many positive, a few negative and debilitating, but I can honestly say that I have never doubted my Call to the Christian Ministry or wished I had done anything else with my life. When one honestly believes oneself to be called by God one can only say 'Yes', and find along the road that the strength is always given for the task – at least, that is my experience.

I suppose all ministers look back on their first pastorate as a time that either made or broke their ministry. Churches that call a minister straight from college have a particular responsibility in this respect, and need to recognise it and set out to support a minister who, after all, has had little experience of this kind of work, especially, as in my case, when he or she is ordained in their twenties. I was immensely fortunate. The Deacons at Arley, mostly old enough to be my parents or even grandparents, were very supportive, even when we had disagreements as we did from time to time. Their names come back to me as I write: Mrs Aitken, Miss Madge, Mrs Pearce, Mr Lennox, Mr Cooper, Mr Evans, Mr Watkins - we used surnames in those days, particularly for people who were older than ourselves. I remember an argument with the Deacons about that very matter, when they had

Ordination July 1960

heard the teenagers in the church calling me by my Christian name. My response was that if I could get respect only by insisting on the use of my surname, then I was not worthy of that respect. But it didn't cut much ice with the Deacons!

The Church Secretary, Ernest Perry, and his wife Joyce were particularly supportive. They were in their mid-forties in 1960 and lived very close to us with their three sons, David, Andrew and Kenneth. Ernest was an experienced Lay Preacher and had also led the young people's work of the church for many years. In some ways, because of his ability and personality, he tended to dominate the congregation, but I found him an immensely loyal colleague and friend. He was a man of vision, experience and maturity and I thank God that he was Church Secretary in the early years of my ministry. As a result of the experience of working with him I have always made a point of cultivating a special relationship with Church Secretaries wherever I have worked. I kept in touch with Joyce and Ernest for the remainder of their lives and was privileged to be asked to conduct their funerals in 1998 and 2000 respectively.

Another deacon at Arley was Helen Pullin, then in her early thirties and a dedicated and successful schoolteacher. A year or two after the commencement of my ministry she came to me after service one Sunday night and told me that she felt a calling to the ordained ministry. It is a comparatively rare privilege for a minister to have such a conversation with a member of the church, and I treasure this first one in my experience. There would be others. Helen trained at what was then New College, London, and was ordained in 1967. We have kept in touch over the years. In retirement after pastorates in Wiltshire, Paignton, Sutton Coldfield and Hampshire, she now lives in Plymouth.

The organist at Arley Chapel was one Pam Keck – an eccentric character if ever there was one. She spent most of her life on some kind of small holding that she owned and would arrive at church on Sundays in clothes more suited to her work than to playing the organ in church. She owned a small dog which she brought with her to choir practice and tied up in the pulpit – much to the annoyance of many of the members of the choir! She was, like many musicians, highly temperamental and you never knew what kind of mood she would be in when she arrived. But she was a highly talented musician and did a great deal to enhance the church's worship by her musical contribution. I have been very fortunate in the organists of the churches where I have ministered. Hilda Tilney in Plymouth regarded her playing as a ministry, and it was. Ernest Rayner and Bill Betterton in Cardiff were likewise committed to their task. Charles Strange, who had reigned from the organ stool in Palmers Green for forty years when I arrived in 1981, though, like Pam Keck. very temperamental, was nevertheless a first class musician and minister of music. After he died in 1985 we were privileged to enlist the services of his son John and also Paul Bateman who were both highly gifted. Paul in particular rose high in his profession, acting as musical director for several West End musical shows, and brought a number of those who participated in those shows to Palmers Green. Others supplemented the contribution these people made on occasion. Organists are an increasingly rare breed, and good organists even more so, as I discover as I move around the churches today to lead their worship. I therefore consider myself to have been immensely fortunate to have worked with such talented people.

In those days in the Congregational Union, local churches were normally expected to pay their minister a stipend which accorded with a minimum agreed by the Union. Some churches were able to offer much more than this. There were some churches, however, who could not afford even to pay the minimum stipend. To assist them, the Congregational Union sponsored what was called the Home Churches Fund, into which all churches were invited to contribute and to which the poorer churches could apply for assistance. This system worked fairly well, and benefited many churches that otherwise would have been without ministry. The almost inevitable consequence, however, was that two classes of pastorate tended to develop: those that were 'independent' and those that were 'on the Fund'. The former were free to pay what they liked over and above the minimum, leading to wide disparity in the remuneration ministers received. The latter, sometimes thought of as 'second class pastorates', tended to attract either ministers straight from college or those whose ability was limited and were unlikely for that reason to be called to the richer churches. Arley was 'on the fund'. It tried annually to lift itself above the threshold, but consistently failed to do so. It did not greatly worry me, however, that I would receive the minimum stipend. At the time of my ordination it was merely £460 a year, but at the age of 25, with only RAF service and University grant behind me, I had never earned so much!

Frances and I had waited five years since our first meeting and two years since we had formally pledged ourselves to each other in engagement to be married. In 1959 she left the Women's Royal Air Force, returned home to High Wycombe and started work as a Comptometer Operator with the furniture manufacturers Ercol. We had spent a good deal of time together, of course, during my time at college, usually travelling to one another's homes for weekend visits and corresponding regularly by letter. There were no e-mails in those days – people wrote letters and put them in the post! Both of us treasured the letters we had received from each other, and kept them until about 1968 when we decided to destroy them – an emotional moment! With the approaching end of my training we started to plan our wedding. It took place on September 10th 1960 in Wesley Methodist Church, High Wycombe, Frances' home church. Their minister, the Revd Eric Firth, presided and the central part of the ceremony, including the vows, was led by my father. My brother Timothy did me the honour of being my best man, Frances's sister, Kathryn, was her 16-year-old bridesmaid and her father, Kenneth Hunt, gave her away. My school friend David Yarrow played the organ. The reception was held in the Church Hall – neither our families nor we had enough money to splash out on a lavish affair. All this took place in the days before people began to arrange a disco to take place in the evening of a wedding day – indeed, discos had not yet been invented! 1960 had been a very cool, wet summer, but that day was warm and sunny – so much so that the icing on the wedding cake melted and the supportive pillars collapsed before the cake was cut! But it was a memorable day. I can recall many of the details even now.

We spent the first weekend of our marriage in a small hotel in Paddington, London, and then travelled to Cornwall for our honeymoon – the first week in the Scilly Isles, the second week in St Ives. We had no car – many people didn't then – so we went by sleeping-car train down to Penzance on the Sunday night. This was luxury! Except that it wasn't, as the bunks in the train were pretty uncomfortable and the noise and motion of the train kept us awake for much of the night! The Scillies, however, proved to be a delectable spot for a honeymoon and we thoroughly enjoyed our stay there in beautiful weather. The weather did not hold for our week in St Ives, but we enjoyed it nevertheless, and returned home to our first manse in time for me to conduct the Harvest Festival services at the end of the month.

Our home was a Georgian house dating from the early part of the 19th Century: very elegant, with very large rooms. It boasted a plaque on the front wall, deriving from the days when every Insurance Company had its own Fire Service and would attend only those houses that were insured with them. We furnished three rooms

Frances and Keith Wedding, September 10 1960

initially, all on the ground floor – a lounge-cum-study, a bedroom and the kitchen. Later we expanded upstairs, mainly utilising second-hand furniture, and created a study in the basement. Floors were mostly stained boards with a small carpet or rug in the centre. These were the days before central heating and double-glazed windows. The draughts were considerable! The winter of 1962/3 was particularly memorable, when we had several feet of snow in Bristol. There has never been so much snow there since! There were six steps up to our front door, and the snow that morning (it was a Sunday) was level from the top step to the top of the front gate. Eventually an ancient snowplough came across the top of our short road, and then across the bottom, leaving piles of snow across both entrances, which then froze and stayed frozen for weeks. Our young son, then eighteen months old, didn't go out of the house for weeks! And inside we lived in our overcoats to keep warm.

These were also the days before refrigerators, washing machines, television sets and cars became universal. We purchased our first TV in 1962 and our first fridge in 1963. Before that there was a slate slab in the pantry that was intended to keep perishable items cool, and we invested in an 'Osokool' – a small plastic cupboard with a saucer-shape indentation on the top to hold cold water which was supposed to keep the contents cold. Our first washing machine was given to us by Frances's mother when she bought a twin-tub: it was a small model made by Hoover with a hand wringer on top to squeeze the water out of the clothes. We didn't purchase our first car until we were in our second pastorate, in 1965. I did my pastoral work on a push-bike (yes, in hilly Bristol!) and latterly on a second-hand NSU Quickly scooter, 49cc, passed on to me by a colleague minister. As a family we walked, or used the buses and trains. Such was our way of life in Bristol in the early 1960s, but we were happy.

A feature of our life, looking back, has been that wherever we have moved, we have always already known someone in the new place who has welcomed us there and enabled us to settle. In Bristol we had come to know Dorothy and Fred Price, the mother and step-father of Peter Yorke, a friend from Cambridge University. I had stayed with them on previous visits to the city and they had offered hospitality to Frances whenever she came to visit me before our marriage. They were in many ways our surrogate parents in Bristol and offered a great deal of support in those early days of our marriage. They remained friends until they died many years later. When we moved to Plymouth we were similarly welcomed by members of the Pilgrim Church whom we had previously met at the South West Pilots Camp.

Later again in Cardiff we already knew the Revd Mary Evans who had been a colleague in the Bristol District and was by then minister at Grand Avenue Church in Ely, and in London we found ourselves living very close to Eli Schofield, who had been our chaplain when we met at RAF Coltishall, and his second wife Mary. Everywhere we went the way seemed to have been prepared for us – a sign perhaps of the rightness of the moves we were making?

At that time there were often unrealistic expectations of ministers' wives – not of husbands, for there were then very few married female ministers. There lingered in the minds of many people the memory of the time when a minister's wife would act as his unpaid curate – and sometimes would be pleased to fulfil that role. Frances quailed at the thought of this, being by nature reserved and reticent to perform any public function. We were, however, very fortunate in the pastorates we served. We made it clear at the outset that Frances was first of all her own person, then my wife, then (later) the mother of our children, then a church member, and she would then fulfil tasks as a member of the church that suited her particular gifts, abilities and availability. Everywhere people seemed to accept this.

Dr Cocks used to tell us in college that one effective way of a minister's wife evading the traditional expectations was to have a baby. 'We had three pastorates' he said, 'and we had a baby in every one of them!' We followed suit! Stephen Jonathan, our firstborn, arrived a few hours after a thunder-storm on July 3rd 1961. Like all our children, he didn't hang about once his birth began. I telephoned Ernest Perry at about 4.30 in the morning. He came in his car and took us to the Bristol Maternity Hospital, and then took me for a ride in the Mendips, dropping me at home at about 7.00. Fathers were not allowed to be present at the birth of their children then. The matron in the hospital had told me to ring at about 10.00 to see how things were going. Soon after I got in, however, the phone rang and I was told that the baby had been born. Our other three children were born at home, lest we should be unable to get to the hospital in time. It proved to be a much more personal and civilised experience.

We were very proud of our baby son who weighed in at 6lb 8oz. Later, my mother told us that she had 'never seen such a scrawny baby', but to us he was wonderful. He soon put on weight and hasn't lost much since! He was almost equally welcome in the church – the first baby to be born to a serving minister throughout that church's history. People took a keen interest, and we were never without babysitters. One in particular, Dorothy Pearce our Church Treasurer, used to come regularly, and for some reason he woke up whenever she was there – a thing he never normally did during the evening. We thought a little encouragement to wake had almost certainly been exercised! But no matter.

Like many wives in those days, Frances did not go out to work much after our marriage. Before Stephen was born she worked part-time in Ernest Perry's office (he worked for the National Health Service Hospital Board), but not afterwards – not, indeed, until we moved to London in 1976. We were, I suppose, among the last couples who assumed the traditional roles of the man being the 'breadwinner' and the wife managing the home. I have no problem with mothers returning to work after the birth of their children so long as proper care for the children is possible, but shall always be grateful that, in our case, Frances chose to be a full-time mother until all our children were at school. How we managed this on our somewhat meagre stipend I'll never know: suffice it to say that Frances was an excellent manager and a prudent shopper. Had she not been, we'd have soon been in debt!

Arley Chapel had a Pilots Company. Pilots was an organisation for children in Congregational Churches, formed in 1936 and sponsored in the early days by the London Missionary Society. It was designed to interest children in the work of the Church overseas, particularly in the South Pacific. My home church in Cambridge had had a company for a while when I was a child. The organisation continues today within the United Reformed Church, and also in a limited way in churches of other denominations, and has developed into a fine church-based, non-uniformed organisation for children of both sexes, thus complementing the work done in many churches by single-sex uniformed organisations like Scouts, Guides and the Brigades. Soon I was drawn into the regional organisation of Pilots, as was Frances, and in 1962 we began to attend and help to organise the South West Pilots Camp which met in schools in various parts of the country each summer. I became leader of this camp ('Camp Dad' as it was then rather quaintly called) and continued to fulfil this role for several years both while we were still in Bristol and later. These camps, regrettably, are no longer held, the victim of modern regulations concerning the use of school buildings and the rigorous leadership checks that are now obligatory. But they fulfilled a crucial role in the development of the discipleship of scores of children, many of whom still look back on their experience with affection and gratitude. I still meet some of these people occasionally after all these years, some of whom are now leaders in their churches, and as a family we developed a number of life-long friendships with people we met at the camps. Among these friends, notably, is Sheila Chambers, who in 1962 was an officer in the company in Westbury, Wiltshire, and became 'Auntie Sheila' to all our children and very much part of our extended family. Every family profits from having a 'maiden aunt' as a confidante and support.

In most of the pastorates where I have served there was a company of Pilots. In Cardiff and then in Palmers Green we also had the range of Scouts and Guides and their different age-group organisations. I have never had direct experience of the Boys and Girls Brigades, though when, in the seventies, I worked at Church House in London, I served on the central Boys Brigade Religious Advisory Panel. I would want to affirm the good work done by these uniformed organisations, particularly when their leaders are members of the local church, but for me the church-centred nature of Pilots, together with the fact that it caters for boys and girls together, gives it distinct advantages.

Further opportunities for ministry in Bristol beyond my local pastorate were either in youth work or on the ecumenical scene. I was invited to become Youth Secretary for the Bristol District of Congregational Churches and immediately was instrumental in setting up what became 'The Bristol Council of Congregational Youth'. There was a committee representing any church that wished to be involved and we organised a number of activities, including a weekend conference in one of the local churches, with participants sleeping in sleeping bags on the church hall floor. Predictably and pleasantly a number of marriage partnerships developed from these activities, and I took part in several wedding services.

In the Cotham area, where Arley Chapel was situated, there existed what was called 'The Octagon Group of Churches'. Bristol had a reputation, fully justified, of being in the forefront of ecumenical activity and the Octagon Group already had a long history. There were eight Churches – hence the name – Anglican, Methodist, Baptist, Presbyterian and Congregational – and joint activities were arranged on a regular basis: Lenten study groups, united worship for the Week of Prayer for Christian Unity, and a regular meeting of the ministers of the different churches. I became the Secretary/Treasurer of this Group and greatly enjoyed putting into practice some of the ecumenical theory I had developed during my time in Cambridge. There was also a lay secretary – Mrs Stephanie Mellor – the mother of six daughters, and a member of the 'highest' of the Anglican Churches in the group. We worked well together, and I am still in touch with her and her husband, Geoffrey, living in retirement in Lowestoft. When we moved away from Bristol in 1964 the Mellors gave me a copy of the 1928 Prayer Book, inscribed 'to a catholic-minded Congregationalist'. I was touched by that. I think we were particularly fortunate in Cotham at that time in the committed leadership we had, both ministerial and lay, and significant progress was made. One joint activity I particularly remember was a coach outing to visit the newly consecrated cathedral in Coventry, a startlingly modern replacement to the one destroyed during the war. I also treasure the memory of the occasion when the Bishop of Bristol, the Right Revd Oliver Tompkins, preached one Sunday evening in Arley Chapel. He was one of the ecumenical giants of those days – whose ancestry included a family of Congregationalists. His uncle, also called Oliver, was martyred with James Chalmers in Papua at the turn of the 19th century. These were years in which the ecumenical movement seemed to be forging ahead and some of us dared to hope that a united Church in Britain was a possibility within our lifetime.

It was while we were in Bristol that I began to attend the annual Assembly of the Congregational Union which always took place in Westminster Chapel in London – a vast auditorium, seating 2,500 people on the ground floor and in the two galleries, one above the other. It was always full. This church was at that time famous for the ministry of Dr Martyn Lloyd Jones, a preacher in the Welsh Calvinist tradition. I heard him preach once, and was inspired even though differing considerably from him theologically. He did not appear, however, at our annual assemblies – the 'May Meetings' as they were popularly called. At the first of these assemblies after I was ordained I was presented, along with about fifty other newly-ordained ministers, to the Chairman. This was a significant moment in my experience. The Chairman that year was the Revd Bert Hamilton, a minister to whom, as I have already mentioned, I always looked up with respect bordering on reverence. I count it a privilege to have been 'received into the Congregational Union' by him. I was always uplifted by attendance at these gatherings. They gave us, especially young ministers in comparatively small churches, what I later heard Dr Kenneth Slack refer to as 'a sense of the multitude'. We were part of something much larger than our own local fellowship, and felt proud to belong. With the advent of the United Reformed Church in 1972 these large assemblies disappeared, but I remember them with great affection.

The sixties were a heady time theologically. In 1963 John Robinson, formerly Dean of Clare College, Cambridge, and my New Testament tutor, now Bishop of

Woolwich, wrote his landmark book 'Honest to God'. It is said that he wrote it while recovering from a bad dose of influenza, which may have coloured his outlook, and what he wrote sent shivers down the spines of many of the more orthodox Christians among us. His thesis was that much of the New Testament must be seen as allegorical rather than literal truth, coming as it does out of an entirely different intellectual and religious context from the one in which we live today. God, he said, is not 'up there' or 'out there' but must be seen as 'the ground of our being', present and accessible. Robinson was really only making accessible the thinking of American and continental theologians like Paul Tillich, who propounded the need to 'demythologise' the Bible. But his book took the theological world by storm and pointed up strongly the difference between Biblical literalists and more radical thinkers. It set the tone for a decade of highly intensive theological debate, spawning, among other influences, a fortnightly radical magazine called 'The New Christian' which many of us eagerly bought and avidly devoured in preparation for our sermons. The debate rumbles on, but sometimes one wishes for the theological dynamism of the sixties.

1963 also brought the international Cuba crisis, when confrontation between Russia and America came closest to bringing the world to the brink of nuclear war. Fortunately for us all the leaders of these two powerful nations, headed by Presidents Kruschev and Kennedy, saw sense and the crisis was defused, but it was a moment when the world held its breath.

Most of us, it is said, can remember exactly where we were when we heard of the assassination of President Kennedy in 1963. There is a steep hill close to Arley Chapel, leading up to the house, which used to be the manse. I was walking up this hill when I met Andrew Perry coming down. It was he who told me the news. I remember being stunned, as was half the world. Kennedy had shown himself to be a charismatic and very effective president for the brief years he had been in office. He had demonstrated outstanding leadership and promised greater things. How the world would have developed had he lived is one of the imponderable questions of history. He was 43. It is sobering to realise that he would have been 88 if he was still alive today.

Towards the end of 1963 I was approached by the Revd Ralph Ackroyd, then minister of Pilgrim Church in Plymouth (and my predecessor as 'Camp Dad' of the South West Pilots Camp) to consider letting my name go forward as prospective minister of the newly established Derriford Church in that city. I was not seeking a move – indeed, as it has turned out, I have never once sought a move throughout my ministry. I have always been approached seemingly 'out of the blue', and have had to respond to initiatives others have taken. Believing as I do that God's will is revealed through the insights of others and of the corporate fellowship of the Church, I have always had to take such approaches seriously. I therefore had to do so on this occasion. As I reflected on the situation, I came to the conclusion that I had perhaps done all I could in the years I had been at Arley. The church had maintained its position membership-wise – many had died and some had moved away during the time I had been there, but others had come to take their places, and the total membership figure was still around the 70 mark as it had been in 1959. I was conscious that the age-profile was high and that change would be inevitable within the next few years, but perhaps it was for someone else to pilot them through that change. I therefore allowed my name to go forward. Frances and I visited Derriford in November 1963, met with the Deacons, had tea with the congregation, and I led worship morning and evening on the Sunday. I made it clear that I would not be in a position to move until the following summer, for reasons that will shortly become apparent. But clearly there was a spark between us during that visit, and soon afterwards I received a unanimous call to move to Plymouth. Again, with my strong belief in the Call of God coming through the declared mind of a congregation, I could do no other than accept.

Having done so, and having made my decision known to the congregation at Arley, we immediately started to review the present life and future opportunities of the church. As it happened (coincidence or divine guidance?) the minister of the neighbouring Cotham Grove Baptist Church, Harry Mowvley, who also taught at the Bristol Baptist College, announced his intention to take up a full-time post at the college during the summer of 1964. We spoke about ecumenical possibilities, and both came to see that maybe there was a reason why we had been led to give much longer notice to our respective pastorates than is customary. We therefore instigated conversations with a view to uniting the two churches into one congregation. Before long the minister of the nearby Cotham Methodist Church heard of our proposals, and his congregation entered the conversations. The result was that, not long after Harry and I finished our ministries there, Christ Church Cotham was born – a union of Baptists, Congregationalists and Methodists, the first three-sided union in the UK. Arley Chapel became redundant and, after a short period, was bought by the Roman Catholic Church for use by the Polish community. Using what had been the Methodist building, Christ Church flourished for about thirty years before, in turn, it came to the conclusion that its mission in that part of Bristol was done. I have always thought that a united Church will come about when people of different denominations locally do all they can to express their God-given unity in their own place, and I was immensely pleased to have been part of these developments in Cotham.

But we were on the move. In July 1964 we pulled up the roots we had put down in Bristol and moved to another pleasant place on the borders of Devon and Cornwall.

Chapter 8
THE FAMILY

In the previous chapter I referred to the arrival of Stephen Jonathan in July 1961. He was followed two years later by Rebekah Mary, born on June 20 1963. Apparently following Dr Cocks' advice, after we moved to Plymouth Christopher James was born on May 20 1967, and, four years later in Cardiff, Judith Rhianon arrived on February 26 1971. We had always hoped for four children, and our hopes were rewarded. We found parenthood to be a challenge but also a great privilege. Fortunately, Frances was a natural mother as well as being a supportive wife, and she was able throughout their childhood to be there for all four of the children, not least when my work took me away from the house and, sometimes, away from home.

Stephen was a slow starter – except for his swift arrival! Instead of crawling, he chose to move around by a complicated shuffling movement on his bottom. Being thus able to see the world in a way crawlers cannot, he didn't get up and walk until he was 19 months old. I remember the day well. We were at church and Stephen was in the crèche, being looked after by Ethel Perry, the sister of our Church Secretary. Ethel couldn't wait to bring him into church after the service and show that he had started walking during the previous hour. Since that time Stephen has always preferred to move at a leisurely pace through life, often waiting for opportunities to drop into his lap rather than going out to look for them. After schooling in Plymouth, Cardiff and Mill Hill in London, he learned to be a Computer Programmer with the Co-op Bank and has remained in computer-related work ever since. In 1992 he and Patricia Slater became a partnership and gave us two lovely grandchildren: Connor Patrick, born on July 16 1995 and Naomi Patricia, born on December 31 1997. They moved from Walthamstow in London to Thornbury near Bristol towards the end of 1995 when Stephen took a post with the National Westminster Bank in the city of his birth, and have become settled there. He currently works for the telephone company Orange. Seeing Connor now at Secondary School, and remembering how grown up I felt when I made the same move 60 years ago, brings home the speed of the passing of time.

Rebekah was born at home in Bristol, and had an even speedier birth than Stephen – indeed, her head was already protruding when the midwife arrived to deliver her, and she was here no more than half an hour later. As she was being born the umbilical cord was wound around her neck, so it was just as well that the midwife had arrived. Rebekah has always been a strong character, and more inclined to active pursuits than to academic ones. Being the second child, she was very competitive with her older brother in her early years. It took Stephen a long time and much effort (on our part as well as his!) to learn to ride a bicycle. Rebekah jumped on his bike one day and immediately rode it down the road! Looking back, it would seem that she was mildly dyslexic at a time when this disability was only beginning to become recognised, and was thus slow to read and study, while showing great artistic talent. She left school in London at the age of 16 and became an apprentice hairdresser in the Army and Navy stores. She quickly became very proficient at her chosen career. In 1992 she moved to the United States, first to Boston and then to New York, to undertake both salon work and training across several states. Currently she is involved with a high–class salon in Manhattan and also with hairdressing for modelling assignments. In 1986 she married Paul Wilson in a ceremony which I conducted in our church in Palmers Green. This marriage, however, ended in 1992 when she moved to the States. In 1994 she married Nikola Matic, a man of Serbian extraction who was brought up in Slough in the UK but had moved to New York, where they met in a gym. After a major operation in 1993 it seemed unlikely that Rebekah would ever be able to have children, but on September 19 1999 Sahara arrived somewhat unexpectedly, and three years later, on May 7 2002, she was joined by Beaufort. Sadly, this marriage too has broken, but Rebekah is doing well as a single working mother, with the daily support of an excellent child-minder. The family continues to live in New York where the children go to school and are involved in many of the activities one expects of children both there and here.

Christopher was our Plymouth baby. He was due a few days before the General Assembly of the Congregational Church was scheduled to start. Obviously it was unthinkable that I should go and leave Frances at such a time. In the event, however, he did not arrive until after the Assembly concluded, so in theory at least I could have gone! Thanks to Christopher this and another Assembly about ten years later are the only two I have so far missed since I was ordained. Christopher was the largest of our four babies, weighing in at 9lb. Interestingly, he is now the slimmest of the four as an adult. Like Stephen he shuffled rather than crawling before he eventually began to walk. More introverted than either of his older siblings, he loves to tell how he bore the brunt of their teasing and took the blame for their misdemeanors as he was growing up. He was three years old when we moved to Cardiff, where he started school, continuing his education in three different schools in London. Both Stephen and Rebekah were Pilots in Cardiff, but Christopher missed out on that, though he did attend the annual camps with his parents. He joined the cubs and the scouts in London. Leaving Minchenden School in Southgate in 1985 he gained entrance to Brunel University where he took a degree in design and technology with education. He has been employed in a number of industrial design companies in London but is currently working on a free-lance basis. At University he met Tonia Graves, later to become a qualified accountant with Price Waterhouse Cooper in the city of London. They married in a lovely ceremony in a splendid Roman Catholic Church in Italy in 1996, Tonia being half-Italian. On October 12 2001 Stella Francesca was born – a lively youngster if ever there was one. Like all her cousins, she has now reached school age. They live in Putney, in south London. It is a deep sadness to us all that Frances knew only Connor and Naomi of the grandchildren, and then only when they were very small. She would have loved knowing all five of them, watching them grow up and sharing in their lives.

Judith was born in our Cardiff manse in 1971 – our Welsh baby, hence her second Christian name: Rhianon. Of all our offspring, she managed to go through her schooling with the least disruption. She began in Cardiff, but we moved to London when she was still in the reception year, and she moved through both Infants and Junior schools in Mill Hill before going to Secondary School in Palmers Green. Academically the most able of our four children, she did not excel at sport. She gained entrance to Newcastle-upon-Tyne University in 1989 to read for a degree in English Literature. Feeling a desire to enter social work, she did a number of unqualified jobs in that general area for a number of years before undertaking a Social Work degree course at Goldsmith's College, University of London. Since then she has worked in Family and Child Care for the London Boroughs of Tower Hamlets and Camden. At college she met Peter Turton, also now a Social Worker, and in 2004 they committed themselves publicly to one another at an unusual but very moving ceremony which I had the privilege of conducting in a 1930s–style ballroom in Lewisham. Currently they live in Camberwell, south London, but spend as much time as they can travelling the world.

Parenting is a demanding, but somewhat chancy business, as parents try to steer a middle course between being over-protective and completely libertarian. The modern world presents opportunities and challenges that make growing up much more complicated than it seems to have been in our day. Frances and I tried to abide by the philosophy propounded by Kalil Gibran in his lovely book 'The Prophet', particularly when he says:

'Your children are not your children. They are the sons and daughters of Life's longing for itself. They come through you but not from you, and though they are with you yet they belong not to you. You may give them your love but not your thoughts. You may house their bodies but not their souls, for their souls dwell in the house of tomorrow, which you cannot visit not even in your dreams. You may strive to be like them, but seek not to make them like you. For life goes not backward nor tarries with yesterday. You are the bows from which your children as living arrows are sent forth'.

Rebekah, Stephen, Christopher and Judith, London 1989

We counted ourselves fortunate that none of our children fell into unsavoury company or destructive habits, and that all of them are in gainful employment and making a responsible contribution to the life of the community. As practising Christians, it saddened us that none of them have identified with the Faith which has always been so important to us. The children of ministers seem either to develop a very deep Christian commitment or fail to espouse it entirely. Ours seem to have taken the latter course and have turned away from the Church in which they were all baptised and reared. This is a continuing disappointment to me, and I frequently chasten myself with my share in the blame. My absence from home in the course of a very busy ministry must have had something to do with it. I believe that the Christian faith has so much to offer them, and furthermore they could be so valuable to a church if they chose to belong. I am also saddened that my five lovely grandchildren are being brought up entirely secularly. But there is little that I can do about that now, especially living a long way from them as I do. But I know that I *'may give them my love, but not my thoughts'* and this I try to do. My family remain a great support to me and a source of much pride and satisfaction.

Sahara (aged 8), daughter of Rebekah and Nik

Beaufort (age 5) 2007. Son of Rebekah and Nik

Connor (aged 10) and Naomi (aged 8),
son and daughter of Stephen and Patricia

Stella age 5, daughter of Christopher and Tonia

Chapter 9
FURTHER WEST – 1964-70

I must return to the chronological account from which I diverged in the previous chapter. Plymouth was quite different from Bristol. Though a city of similar size, it had a slower pace of life. We discovered that its motto tended to be ' don't put off until tomorrow what you can put off until the day after'! Almost the whole of the centre of the city had been destroyed by enemy action during the second World War and much of it had been rebuilt during the fifties and early sixties. The new building, however, had been accomplished when materials were restricted and even then was beginning to show signs of wear. I understand that many buildings have now been demolished and replaced in a more modern idiom. We had been called to a new church in a new area of development some four miles from the city centre. Formerly, before the city expanded, there had been a number of large houses bordering a main road and among them there was a small wooden non-denominational mission hall known as Down House Mission. Feeling the need to draw on the resources of one of the main line denominations so that it could serve the burgeoning area more effectively, it had become recognised as a Congregational Church in 1955. In 1963, by a supreme effort on the part of the 30 members, it had declared itself independent of the Home Churches Fund and undertaken to provide the minimum stipend locally and to seek a minister. So it was to this pioneering congregation that we came in September 1964.

The manse the church had bought for us was in the older part of the neighbourhood – a pleasant 1930s detached property. As Plymouth was radically different from Bristol, so Derriford Church was very different from Arley Chapel. Here, the congregation was almost entirely made up of young and middle-aged couples with their children. In the six years we were there I conducted only two funerals of church members, and only one of them was an elderly person. The kind of housing surrounding the church attracted middle-class executive people, used to exercising responsible leadership in their daily lives. They brought these abilities and lots of ideas with them to church – and sometimes disagreed profoundly! It was quite demanding for me, at the age of barely 30, to try to guide them in their decision-making. Another difference from Arley was that most of these people had scant knowledge of Congregationalism and little desire to learn more. They came from a variety of denominational backgrounds, and in some cases from none. This was the church nearest to where they lived, which suited them as families to attend, and that was what mattered to them. There was thus little or no tradition upon which to build. Instead, we were making our own tradition and it was both exhilarating and scary.

These days, few denominations would consider planting churches in new areas unilaterally. Over the past few decades many new fellowships have been established in new areas ecumenically. We, in what has now become the United Reformed Church, cooperate most often with our Methodist cousins, and there are over 300 places in the country where united churches between our two denominations witness to the faith that unites us, many of them in new areas. It was rarely done this way in 1964. Instead, churches like Derriford were established by one denomination who would then encourage people from other backgrounds and none to attend, Other denominations, by mutual agreement, would refrain from moving into that area. Thus, though we were technically a Congregational Church, we were in reality an ecumenical congregation.

There was considerable growth as the neighbourhood expanded. The sixties were a decade when many people who moved into a new area often sought out a church to which to belong. Ours was, to all intents and purposes, the Parish Church of the area, and a number of the new residents came to worship with us. There were 30 members when we arrived. When we left in 1970 there were 77, but of the original 30 only 9 remained – the measure of the movement in and out of the district. The records show that we had 130 children - more than there have been in any other church of which I have been minister. Very quickly we needed to do something about our premises, which were restricting our growth. To cut a very long story short, in December 1966 a fine new building was opened on a very central site in the community, costing all of £16,000! The money was raised by the church members and supplemented by some war-damage money ported from a church in the city that was not rebuilt. In design, the building is octagonal and within it the pews (which came from another church in the city that was redundant) are arranged in semi-circles around the central pulpit, communion table and font: in other words, it is a modern version of a 17th century dissenting meeting house. It seats about 120 and very soon was full to overflowing on Sunday mornings. A church hall was added before we left in 1970.

One of the features of Derriford Church was that it attracted a considerable number of intelligent grammar school students, many of them encouraged to come by our Church Secretary, Henry Whitfeld, who had taught all his life at Devonport High School for Boys, and his wife Marjorie who taught at St Dunstan's School for Girls. Mostly these young people attended the evening service, some of them travelling considerable distances by bus to do so. After the service they would gather for intense discussion in the manse or in the homes of other church members. These discussions often took me into deep waters. I often wonder whether the members of the group realised how much I floundered some of the time! But they presented a wonderful evangelistic opportunity. I have lost touch with most of them, but Stephen Wyatt who teaches in Felixstowe still communicates at Christmas, and has been kind enough to comment more than once on how much he owes to his time at Derriford; David Tatem has been a minister of the United Reformed Church since 1979; and Brian Harvey lives now not far from me in North Wales and is a non-stipendiary priest in the Church in Wales while working also as secretary to the St Asaph Diocese.

It was not long before I was asked to exercise wider aspects of ministry in the city and district. For a time I served as Chairman of the Plymouth Congregational Council and as Secretary of the Plymouth Council of Churches. Not long before we moved from Plymouth I was elected Chairman of the Southern Division of the Congregational County Union. This was also the one and only time in my ministry when I served as a Free Church Hospital Chaplain, at Greenbank Hospital in central Plymouth, as well as being chaplain of the Crownhill Convalescent Home near the church. For a short while I also did some RE teaching in Devonport High School for Girls.

We enjoyed living in Plymouth. Here we both learned to drive and bought our first car – a little black Austin A35. This and subsequent vehicles enabled us to explore the lovely Devon coastline and Dartmoor, both on our doorstep. There was no need to travel far for holidays, especially with young children, as there were beautiful beaches near at hand. The only drawback to living there was that Plymouth is very much on the end of the country, and our families lived in Buckinghamshire and Suffolk. In the days before motorways, it would take us 13 or 14 hours to drive to Ipswich, with at least one child who was regularly travelsick and another who habitually enquired whether we were 'there yet' when we had gone no further than the end of the road! But the delights of the area where we lived amply compensated.

In 1965 we acquired the only dog we have ever had as a family. The neighbour of a member of our congregation had a bitch who had presented her with a litter of six. One or two only remained and she was anxious to find them a home. Thus we became the owners of Candy, thus named because when she was a puppy she had white, brown and black striped legs! She was a cross between a beagle and a labrador: an interesting mixture that made her temperamentally ideal for a family with children. She was much loved by us all. She came with us on holidays and on visits to friends, and she moved with us to Cardiff and later to London. Sadly, she had a stroke and died just before we moved from Mill Hill to Palmers Green in London in 1981, but at 16 she was a good age. The children were anxious that we should replace her, but we decided that dogs could be a tie, especially as Frances and I would undoubtedly be left with the dog when the children left home. Under pressure, however, we took on two kittens, Sugar and Spice, in 1982. They quickly became part of the family and remained so until just before I retired from Manchester. I remember how odd it felt at first, after they had died, to come into the house and not be met by a living creature. But, with the lifestyle I have developed since I retired, being away from home a good deal, it would not be kind to have an animal. So I content myself with the fish in my garden pond!

Stephen and Rebekah started school in Plymouth: Widey Infants School in nearby Crownhill. Asked when he came home after his first day there whether he had enjoyed it, Stephen said that he had – 'but we didn't learn to read'! After a while we moved them to Whitleigh School nearer home. Stephen also began to have piano lessons and seemed to enjoy them at least initially. Rebekah went down the same route for a short period after we moved to Cardiff, but her teacher suggested that we were wasting her time and our money, so she gave it up!

One of the community activities we sponsored was a Play Group in the days when this kind of provision was in its infancy. Iris Watson, a church member, and a group of helpers ran the scheme which was very successful in serving the many young families in the neighbourhood and (though this was never the motive in sponsoring the scheme) in recruiting some of them to attend church services.

It was while we were living in Plymouth that we witnessed an event that, in its way, went down into history. In 1967 we went down to Plymouth Hoe to see Sir Francis Chichester arrive in the Sound on his yacht 'Gypsy Moth', having circled the world single-handed without a stop – the first person to do so. It was impressive, seeing how small was the boat and knowing how vast was the ocean and how great the distance. The boat has been preserved and is on display in Greenwich.

Another and more momentous event in the history of the world took place while we were in Plymouth – in 1969. One clear night I remember standing in the church car park, looking up at the moon and trying to take in the fact that at that very moment Buzz Aldrin and Neil Armstrong were walking on its surface. As children we had sung the song 'The man in the moon came down too soon' but never did we expect that we'd witness men going there. As I stood and looked I remembered how my father, then 71, had told me how as a lad with his father he had seen the first motor cars drive past the Royal Exchange in London, and now, in his lifetime, he and his contemporaries had seen men travelling to the moon. So much change and development in such a comparatively short time. I wondered what changes I might see in my own lifetime. As I write I am now the same age as my father was then, and the list of inventions and developments since I was born in 1935 is enormous. Yet somehow, as human beings, we adapt to them, just as my father adapted to the news of space travel. A few months after this epoch-making event I was asked to baptise a baby – with the name Neil Armstrong! I wonder where that 38 year-old man is now?

In 1970 Plymouth celebrated the 350th anniversary of the sailing of the Pilgrim Fathers to America – their final port of call in Britain had been Plymouth. It fell to me, as Secretary to the Council of Churches, in partnership with the ever-energetic Henry Whitfeld, to organise a massive procession of witness down Armada Way and up on to the Hoe. Many hundreds came for what proved to be a worthy celebration, reminding the Plymouth public that the Pilgrim Fathers had embarked upon what was essentially a quest for religious freedom.

Looking back I can see that the Plymouth ministry was 'ministry on the run'. Ministering with a new church, rapidly expanding, getting involved in its community, contacting new residents, building up its corporate life, harnessing all kinds of new ideas was, if I am honest, leaving us all rather breathless. In the 38 years since we left, the neighbourhood has settled down, there are fewer young people around, those young residents who have remained have become middle-aged, even elderly, a good many of those who were leaders in the church have died, and our lovely new building is showing signs of wear. Theologically, succeeding ministers have differed from my approach, and recently the church has become much more informal in its worship and conservative in its theology. Bu the church is still there, serving the community. I shall always be pleased that I had a major share in its inception.

Six strenuous years were interrupted by a phone call one evening in November 1969 from someone who announced himself as 'Frank Bucknall, secretary of Roath Park Congregational Church in Cardiff'. As soon as I heard his voice I somehow knew what he was going to say and in my heart knew what the outcome was likely to be. The Deacons there had been given my name as a prospective minister. I visited Cardiff to meet them and to explore possibilities, and the atmosphere in the meeting confirmed my original premonition. They invited me to visit more formally and to lead worship in January 1970. Again all the signs were positive. At first, though I was fairly sure that the unanimous Call that came from the subsequent Church Meeting was of God, and that I should accept, I could not convince myself that my work in Plymouth was complete. It took a much older and wiser minister, the Revd Frank Quick, in active retirement worshipping as a member of our congregation, to help me to see my way forward. In his simple and direct way, he said 'My dear Keith. If it is God's will for you to go to Cardiff it must be God's will for you to leave Plymouth'. In my arrogance I had perhaps been thinking that I was needed in both places. I therefore accepted the Call, though, as when I was moving from Bristol to Plymouth, I asked them to delay my coming until the end of July so that I could lead the Derriford Church to the completion of the building of its church hall. Thus it was that our pilgrimage was once again disturbed as we prepared to move.

Chapter 10
TO WALES – 1970-76

Roath Park was as different in many respects from Derriford as Derriford had been different from Arley. Arley was more or less 'inner-city' to use a jargon that has become well-used since we were there. Derriford was outer suburb. Roath Park was between the two. The church had been built in 1897 to serve a rapidly developing residential area. The congregation came from the streets of late Victorian terraced housing around the church and from the very affluent suburb of Cyncoed on the surrounding hills. At the centre of the area was Roath Park itself, a long narrow lung in the closely built-up area, offering spacious lawns, a boating lake, tennis courts, rose gardens, children's playgrounds and, at one end, a wild area. The manse was situated opposite these wild gardens.

We had imagined Cardiff to be a mixture between coal mines and docks. How wrong we were! Yes, there were still many coal mines operating in the valleys to the north of the city, and the docks were still in operation, carrying Welsh coal to foreign parts. But the city itself was impressive, pleasant and vibrant, with magnificent shops, a strong commercial life, the offices of a capital city and a major branch of the University of Wales. Furthermore, to the north, beyond the industrial belt, lay the wonderful countryside of the Brecon Beacons which we gradually explored. While we were there communication with the rest of the country improved dramatically with the opening of the M4 motorway. A visit to the city today reveals that all these features have developed considerably, with new shopping centres and pedestrianised streets in the centre and the amazing new development in Cardiff Bay. We soon realised that we had been called to yet another pleasant place in which to live.

When we agreed to move to Cardiff no one told us that we would feel as if we had entered a foreign land. We soon found out that we had! The Welsh culture permeated civic and church life, even in cosmopolitan Cardiff. Over the centuries, we discovered, Wales had been oppressively subjugated by England both industrially and politically. As a result there was a suspicion of anything English and of English people moving in, especially if they tried to impose English ways of dealing with Welsh concerns. No one had prepared me for this. Fortunately I have always believed that ministers, in any situation, should take time when they first arrive in a new pastorate to take the temperature, to get to know people, and to gain people's trust before embarking on any new departures. Looking back, I am very glad that I took my own advice in Roath Park. Other English ministers coming in to Wales did not always fare so well. We enjoyed living and working in the capital of Wales, and made many friends, but in some ways it felt strange for the whole of our time there.

This strangeness had its fascination, focussed on the prevalence of the Welsh language. We knew, of course, that it was still a living language, but had not expected it to have such a high profile. Following a period when it had been illegal to be heard to be speaking Welsh in public, great efforts were now being made to revive and develop its use. The road signs were all bi-lingual. Every government form, from the tax return to the TV licence, came in two languages. Welsh nationalists were on the march. Second homes in west Wales, owned by English people, were being torched. Civil protest, often led by nonconformist ministers and church members, was very evident. There were many Welsh-speaking churches around – indeed, we learned that for decades it had been the churches who had kept the language alive when its use had been frowned upon in the wider community. All children, ours included, were expected to learn Welsh in school, and even in Cardiff there were schools where the education was done in the medium of Welsh. These schools were eagerly sought-after, especially by middle-class families who believed that the education would be superior to that offered by the English schools. We had no problem with much of this – except when we were made to feel a little like second-class citizens because of our lack of knowledge of the language. Monoglot English-speaking Welsh people sometimes felt this even more keenly than those coming in from elsewhere.

I mentioned that the pace of life in Plymouth was noticeably slower than what we had been used to in Bristol. In Cardiff we noticed a reluctance to deal with persistent problems. The historical subjugation by the English found expression in a tendency to complain and whinge, but a reluctance to do anything about it. This tendency sometimes affected the life of the Church, to the impairment of its witness. Church life generally was still greatly affected by the past, not least by the aftermath of the Evan Roberts revival of 1904, when chapels of every hue were erected and, for a time, the chapel reigned supreme in every community. Lurid stories were told of chapels built by the owners of rival collieries and steelworks which the workers were expected to attend for Sunday worship – or risk losing their jobs on Monday morning. Two world wars, the 1930s slump, changes in working conditions, and the emigration of many people of working age into England when there was little work to be found in Wales, had decimated many of the non-conformist congregations. In every community there were now far too many chapels, competing for a much smaller number of willing worshippers. This decline, coupled with a tendency to resist change, was having a debilitating effect in many valley communities and beginning also to affect congregational life in the city. Today, returning to Wales after 25 years absence, I sometimes find the same attitude lingering among even smaller congregations. The tiny congregations that sometimes remain cling on even more tenaciously to their building, their abiding symbol of security in a rapidly changing world. Sometimes these buildings seem to have conditioned their faith to such an extent that they seem unable to conceive of Christianity without them.

Roath Park church was then quite large – about 250 members and 100 children, with a good sprinkling of all age groups. Most people had a grounding in Congregationalism, though for many it was filtered through the interpretation given to it by the Revd R E Salmon who had ministered there from 1913 until 1953. In 1970 he was still affectionately remembered by a large proportion of the congregation. So well-known was he in the community that the church was still sometimes referred to as 'Salmon's Chapel'. His style of ministry was independent, authoritarian and paternalistic. Church Meetings were held no more often than once a year. The Deacons, nominated by him, ruled, but he was in charge. As long as he was there, people acceded to his authority because they knew no other way and they loved him. But when he died, and the Revd Glanville Jones was called to be minister, and he tried to guide the church into more orthodox Congregational ways, great tensions emerged. These had largely subsided by the time we arrived, mostly due to the enabling ministry of the Revd Douglas Bale my predecessor, but the folk memory remained.

It was while we were in Cardiff that the United Reformed Church came into being. English Presbyterians and Congregationalists had increasingly been working and, in a number of places, worshipping together since 1947, when a scheme to unite the two denominations had failed to gain sufficient support. I vividly recall a visit paid to the Congregational Annual Assembly in 1966 by the then Moderator of the Presbyterian Church, the Revd Peter McCall, who had been my near neighbour and colleague in Bristol. He came to make a formal request to us to enter new negotiations with a view to union. The request was enthusiastically agreed, and in 1972, after protracted discussions, the union took place. It was sealed by a meeting of the Assemblies of the two Churches in Westminster Central Hall, London, on October 5, followed later in the day by a great service of thanksgiving and commitment in Westminster Abbey. I was present as a representative at both events: it was a high point in my ministry and the inspiration of the occasion has never left me. Sadly, not all Congregational churches came into the new Church. Each local church had to vote to come in by a prescribed majority, and some two hundred churches did not achieve this. Presbyterian churches, however, with a different ecclesial and legal structure, had to take a positive vote to stay out of the new Church if they wished, and only three did: in Berwick on Tweed, Jersey and Guernsey. Somewhat bizarrely the two Presbyterian churches in the Channel Islands decided to join the Church of Scotland. The one in Berwick, more understandably, made the same decision. I was surprised, and still am, that so many of the English Congregational Churches in Wales voted to join. There were, after all, only three congregations of the Presbyterian Church of England in Wales at the time: two in Cardiff and one in Swansea, so most of our people had little or no experience of English Presbyterianism. Furthermore, the Presbyterian Church of Wales, then very numerous and influential among Welsh non-conformists, was not involved in the conversations or in the new Church. Many of the English speaking Congregational churches, however, did achieve the required majority, including the one where I ministered in Roath Park. It was a historic moment for us all. Many of us fondly hoped that we were ploughing a furrow that others would follow. Indeed, I cherish the memory of the Archbishop of Canterbury Michael Ramsey, speaking in the joint meeting of the two Assemblies after the vote to unite had been taken, saying in his speech that this was one of the most memorable moments in his life. I also remember him, the Archbishop of Westminster Cardinal Heenan and the Moderator of the Free Church Council, as part of the liturgy of the service in the Abbey, pledging to follow where we were leading. For a time it really looked as if something like that would happen, as Anglicans, Methodists and ourselves formed the Churches' Council for Covenanting. A scheme to bring about a new relationship, however, was turned down in 1981 by the Anglicans – to the great relief, it has to be said, of those in the United Reformed Church who had conscientiously voted against it. Since then further unions have taken place – with some of the Churches of Christ in 1981 and with some congregations of the

Congregational Union of Scotland in 2000 – but no plans for a wider national union have been tabled. The search for organic unity has gone on to a back burner, though in many places Local Ecumenical Partnerships have come into being. Thus the fond hope and dream of some of us at university in the 1950s has not been realised, as we had anticipated, in our lifetime, and I and others like me will die disappointed.

Another disappointment for me was the failure of a scheme for local union in which I was heavily involved. Following the coming into being of the United Reformed Church, conversations were initiated in Roath Park to bring together two former Congregational Churches (Roath Park and Minster Road), one former Presbyterian Church of England (St Andrew's) and the Roath Park Methodist Church. In 1974 proposals were considered separately by all four churches. The Methodists agreed. St Andrew's agreed provided that the united church used its buildings. Minster Road turned the proposal down, and our own church failed to come to a clear decision. What soured the situation for me was that I discovered that opposition to the proposals was being fostered behind the scenes. Furthermore, I found out that the United Reformed Church Moderator, who had chaired the discussions, belonged to the same Masonic Lodge as these dissentients and had being doing nothing to challenge the dissent. I therefore felt very let down both by the moderator and by these negative church members. What also both saddened and angered me was that these people were not those who bore the main responsibility of leadership in the church, but always turned up when radical decisions for change were on the agenda, and consistently voted against any such proposal. The committed leaders were all in favour of the changes proposed, but were thus prevented from leading the church in the direction they honestly thought it should go. It was not an easy time. What is even more saddening is to see what has happened in Roath Park since that fateful day in 1974 when the scheme foundered. The Methodist Church has closed and its prominent building on a corner site has become a cheap clothing market. Minster Road Church united with another United Reformed Church later but is only a shadow of its former self. St Andrew's Church continues, but, ironically for a Church in the Presbyterian tradition, in a very independent fashion. And the membership of the church where I ministered has shrunk from over 200 when I left to less than 30 today.

Despite this setback, I continued to minister there for another two years. I became closely involved in the wider life of the United Reformed Church, serving on the

General Assembly's Church Life Department Central Committee and its Youth Committee, and continuing to serve, as I had done for a number of years, on the central Pilots' Panel.

Within the congregation and in the wider community of Roath Park there were many elderly people living alone. I had encountered the Abbeyfield Society in other places and suggested that we might form a branch in Cardiff. We set about doing so, and I became the first Chairman. We purchased our first house not far from the church for the princely sum of £8,500 and set about converting it to a home for six elderly people and a housekeeper. It was a proud moment when the house was opened by the Lord Lieutenant of the County in 1974. Subsequently the Society opened another house round the corner, sponsored by the local Baptist Church, in 1976.

Also in 1974 we had the privilege of welcoming to Cardiff some of the Asian people who had been expelled from Uganda by the ruthless dictator, Idi Amin. We were asked by the local organisers to clean and furnish an empty house close to the church for one of these families. and we did so. I think we were all touched by the gratitude and sense of relief in the hearts of the family who moved in. I sometimes wonder what happened to them, and where those who were children then are now – in their thirties and forties of course.

Summer holidays in our Cardiff years were mostly spent in New Quay, Cardiganshire, where our Church Treasurer, Stewart Wright, and his wife Bess, owned a cottage. This delightful resort, with its safe sandy beach, and the lovely countryside around are still remembered by our children. For us, living on a limited income, it offered important opportunities for family fun in return for very modest expenditure – an ideal combination for cash-strapped ministers!

In 1976 there came yet another of those approaches 'out of the blue'. I was invited to go to London to be interviewed for the post of Secretary for Christian Education and Children's Work at Church House. Following the interview, I was asked to take the post. Remembering my personal philosophy that when one is unexpectedly asked by the Church to consider a move, one ought to give it serious consideration, I duly did so. It was not an easy move to contemplate. It involved leaving local pastoral responsibility, something no minister should do easily, and a move I had always said I would never contemplate. It also involved moving our four children, two of whom were now teenagers and putting down strong roots in the local community. We came to the conclusion, however, that the children's disturbance would not be too damaging for them and that it was probably the right time for me to leave Roath Park, having given them two years' service since the failure of the unity talks. Our last service at Roath Park therefore took place in April 1976 and we moved to suburban London.

Chapter 11
TO LONDON – 1976-81

It did not prove any easier to leave Cardiff in 1976 than it had been to leave Bristol in 1964 or Plymouth in 1970. Friendships born out of close working together in the life of the Church can never be quite the same again after a move, and, for the well-being of the church being relinquished, there is no way a minister who has left should try to maintain them at a close level. I suffered in one church from a predecessor who did his best to maintain intimate contact, and sometimes knew what was happening there before I did. So I have always been careful, having left a post, to put clear water between us. One particular friendship from Cardiff days has, however, persisted. Peter and Pat Linsey were close to us then and remain so. 25 years ago they moved from Cardiff to Chester in the course of Peter's work, and I see them still with some regularity.

The move to London proved to be complicated. There was no house for us, and we seemed to be expected to find one ourselves within a certain very limited price range. Eventually, through the help of others, one was found in Mill Hill, on the very edge of London. It cost £23,000. It was not ideal. It provided the requisite accommodation, however, only because it had two small extra bedrooms built into the loft. This gave us enough space upstairs but only limited space downstairs, just at a time when our family needed more and more room for comfort. In its favour was the fact that by using the railway station at Mill Hill Broadway I could travel easily to St Pancras and thus to the nearby Church House where my office was located.

We hoped that moving out of a local pastorate would have a positive effect upon our children from the church perspective. They would no longer be 'the Manse family', with all that that sometimes entails about exposure and expectations. Unfortunately, however, we found ourselves members of a church where the minister was hardly our kind of man, and gradually Stephen and then Rebekah ceased to attend. I shall always wonder whether, if we had remained in Cardiff, they might have continued into adult church membership. But we shall never know.

Moving teenagers from one place to another is fraught with difficulty, as we soon discovered. The roots they put down in a locality go very deep. After the initial shock of being told of the move, Stephen settled comparatively easily into the new surroundings and into his new school, even though it turned out to be a poor school from many points of view. The move proved to be much more disturbing, however, to Rebekah. At 13 she had not wanted to move from Cardiff, and blamed both me and God for our doing so. She behaved badly both at home and at school, and there was one occasion when she went missing on a Sunday afternoon and eventually telephoned us from Paddington Station when she discovered she did not have enough money for the rail fare to Cardiff. She did not make good friendships at the new school, and frequently found herself in all kinds of trouble. Her dyslexia and the school's failure to understand this did not help. All in all it was good for her when, in 1979, she left school and started her hairdressing apprenticeship. Christopher and Judith, at 9 and 5, soon settled into a small primary school down the road from our house.

Moving to London created unforeseen economic problems for us. In Cardiff we had been receiving the minimum recommended stipend, but such was its level that we received supplementary help including free school meals, free prescriptions and free glasses – and we didn't pay Income Tax. Coming to London, the stipend was greater than the minimum, but this brought us into the Tax bracket and took us out of the free allowance zone. This, coupled with the greater cost of living in London, meant that no longer could we make ends meet. Frances decided to seek part time employment. First she did some domestic work at John Grooms Centre for Disabled People not far from home. Then she underwent a 'return to work' course in secretarial work and book-keeping, for which a grant was available, and subsequently took a part time job in an estate agent's firm where the principal was a fellow church member, John Neal. This proved to be a very good move, both for her and for the family. The economic strains were removed and Frances found new fulfilment in the work.

One useful side-effect of our move to London was that we now lived closer to both our sets of parents. Hitherto we had had to allocate some of our annual holiday to visit them, and, having driven long distances, felt that we had to stay for at least a week to justify the journey. As the children grew up, and the grandparents grew older, this presented both logistical difficulties and an increasing burden on both the grandparents and the parents, to say nothing of the children! Now we were near enough to Frances's people in Buckinghamshire and to mine in Ipswich to visit for a day. Sometimes we said that when we reached retirement we'd try to live near enough to our children to be able to do the same. Things have not worked out that way, however, since I retired to North Wales and the family live in London, Bristol and New York!

Looking back, I have mixed feelings about the work to which I had committed myself. I am glad of the experience it gave me of commuting to a city office – though am now even more glad that I no longer have to do it! I am glad for the exposure it gave me to the wider life of the Church, my own and others, which stood me in good stead for present and future ministry. I am glad that it enabled me to make what I hope was a good contribution to the life of the Church in the area of work for which I was appointed. But it did not yield the satisfaction that work in a local pastorate had afforded. Part of the job entailed leading Church Weekends in various parts of the country. This inevitably meant close working relationships with those congregations, both in the planning and the carrying out of the engagement. But when it was over, I had to disengage from that community and start immediately to engage with another, and never saw the long-term outcome of what had taken place. I found this frustrating. For the rest of the work I always felt myself to be at one stage removed from the real action – which, of course, I was.

I worked as a member of the Church Life Department team, headed by the Revd Robert Latham. Robert had been in central office appointments for almost the whole of his ministry, and he was then nearing retirement. Under a somewhat pompous appearance and manner he had a deeply pastoral heart and was a splendid leader of the team. I grew very fond of him. Other members of the departmental team were the Revd Michael Davies, Youth Secretary, and the Revd Charles Meachin, Secretary for Stewardship. Michael, who became Moderator of Thames North Synod, was succeeded by the Revd John Oldershaw during the time I was there. These two colleagues have remained friends over the years.

For the first time in my life I now had a secretary: Betty Taylor, whose husband, John, was then minister at Beckenham in Metropolitan Kent. This was a new experience, for me and for her, but we both survived! Betty was a strong support, taking a deep personal interest in the work. She often said that she was glad when I was away from the office for a period, either working away or on holiday, so that she could get on with her work uninterrupted! I could not have accomplished half of what I did without her. Betty and John have lived in Minehead since John retired in 1987 and we have remained friends over the years.

The work of my post included developing the all-age approach to worship and education in the life of the Church. A study and action pack was prepared entitled 'Together' and it was my task, having done much of the preparation of the pack, to sell it to the constituency and to use it in many places. It was a natural development of the 'Family Church movement' which had been pioneered by people like the Revd Bert Hamilton, the Revd Dick Hall and Miss Connie Parker during the war years and immediately afterwards. At its core was the belief that children are not the Church of tomorrow, needing to be nurtured accordingly, but are a valid and vital part of the Church of today, with much to contribute as well as much to gain. After all these years I still find people taking the former view and having to be corrected! Did it – does it – work? The number of children in our churches was declining rapidly in 1976 and this trend has continued inexorably, so in that sense it has been a failure. But where it has been developed by ministers and leaders with vision and enthusiasm it is working still, so there has been some success.

Another part of my work was to represent the United Reformed Church on the Board of the ecumenical curriculum material 'Partners in Learning' which was firmly based on the all-age approach. I enjoyed this, though the writing of material for publication, and the editing of the work of other writers, was painstaking and demanding. The material was published annually from 1967 until 2000. I worked with it from 1972 until the mid 1980s, both while at Church House and before and after. It has now been superseded by 'Roots'. I am glad to have been involved in this ecumenical educational programme during its long life.

'Partners in Learning' was published by the National Christian Education Council – an inter-denominational agency for Christian education that had succeeded the once prestigious National Sunday School Union. This body had a dual function: it offered training and support to those involved in the education of children and young people in churches of many denominations, and it published a wide range of books and other teaching aids. I was drawn into its work by virtue of the post I held and I represented the United Reformed Church on its Board. I continued to do so long after moving back into a local pastorate in 1981 – indeed, I served the organisation for about twenty years altogether, and acted as President for a significant period. During that time many changes took place, dictated in part by the changing scene in local churches. In the early 1990s the headquarters moved from Redhill in Surrey, where we had owned a large but wasteful mansion, to Selly Oak in Birmingham, where we were able to work closely with Westhill College across the road. Westhill, one of the Selly Oak Colleges, had itself been founded to train Sunday School teachers, though it had now greatly expanded to become a training college for day-school teachers. In time, the contraction of children's work in the churches made the work of the NCEC less and less viable, and a union with the Christian Education Movement, which serviced religious education in day schools, took place. The new body is now called simply 'Christian Education' and I have lost touch with its work. I realise now, however, if I did not always realise it then, that it was a great privilege to share in this aspect of ministry for so long.

I had not been at Church House long before I was asked to add the work of 'Master Pilot' to my brief. Having been involved in the Pilots movement for so long – in all three pastorates and, indeed, as a child at Emmanuel Church in the 1940s - I was glad to take up this responsibility. It involved acting as executive officer for the movement and keeping oversight of its material. During my time Pilots went through a major review and overhaul, a process which has continued to take place at regular intervals since. It delights me that for the past number of years a full-time development officer has been appointed – Karen Bulley, a product of the South West Pilots Camp – and that the movement has gone from strength to strength at a time when many other aspects of church work have declined.

At the request of my colleague Michael Davies, I had some involvement in the denomination's Youth Work. In particular, on a couple of occasions I took part in one of the national activities of the Youth Committee: 'Anchors Aweigh' – an Easter holiday activity for about 100 young people on boats on the Norfolk Broads. On the first occasion I skippered a boat and on the second occasion led the educational project. I found these activities immensely rewarding. Stephen came with me on these adventures and for a time also got himself involved in another of the national activities organised by the Youth Committee in those days: 'Adventure Camp', held during the summer holidays. With others I greatly regret the demise of these activities that offered so much to the development of young people in our Church.

Another excursion into young people's work was when, soon after I started at Church House, I responded to an invitation to lead a youth weekend at the High Leigh Conference Centre in Hertfordshire for the Thames North and Eastern

Synods. The theme that had been chosen (remember, this was 1977) was '1984' and the whole of the Saturday was given over to acting out the kind of situation featured in George Orwell's book of that name, applying it to the Christian Faith under simulated persecution circumstances. I was cast as 'Big Brother', issuing increasingly restrictive orders to the members from an invisible secret headquarters, using a number of 'pigs' as messengers and informants. It was a memorable time and evoked much serious reflection during a time of de-briefing towards the end of the weekend. Later I took the same format to another youth weekend in Surrey.

While I was at Church House an ecumenical organisation for adult education was formed: the Christian Association for Adult and Continuing Education. I was the United Reformed Church's representative on the committee. This got me involved not only nationally but internationally too. I attended conferences in Holland and Switzerland and enjoyed these experiences even though I am unsure how much of what I did greatly enhanced the life and experience of the Church I represented! I also represented my Church ecumenically on educational committees sponsored by the then British Council of Churches, including the Consultative Group for Ministry among Children – another enlarging experience for me.

From 1977 until 1981 I was responsible for the organisation of the United Reformed Church's annual Forum which took place at the Swanwick Conference Centre in Derbyshire. It had taken place for many years, originally as an activity of the Congregational Church, and drew together church members, young people and children for what was labelled 'a holiday conference'. This event (it still continues) was a deeply spiritual experience for many people, and very good fun too. I am grateful that this came under my care for five years and for all the opportunities it gave me, and my family who always came with me. It was at the first of these Forums that we attended that we became friendly with Clem and Betty Frank. Clem was the newly appointed Financial Secretary of the United Reformed Church, and though he and Betty were Methodists, recently arrived home from a tour of duty as Methodist missionaries in what was then Rhodesia, he played a full part in the life of the United Reformed Church for all the 25 years he served us in this capacity. Our friendship has lasted now for thirty years and we have taken holidays together on many occasions – the mark of true friendship.

When I began in this post and attended ecumenical gatherings of educationists I felt quite inadequate. I had been trained in theology and had some pastoral experience, but the jargon talked with great confidence by these professionals meant little to me and left me cold. Gaining confidence, however, I started occasionally asking them what they meant by what they were saying. Often I discovered that the jargon meant little to them either – an object lesson in clarity of expression – that is, saying what you mean and meaning what you say!

Towards the end of my time at Church House preparations were being made to unify the United Reformed Church and the Churches of Christ, a smaller Protestant denomination in Britain. As this was happening, one of their ministers (the Revd John Oldershaw) was appointed to be Youth Secretary for both denominations and I was asked to extend my Christian Education brief to include the Churches of Christ. The unification took place in 1981 in Birmingham. Once again, as with the inauguration of the United Reformed Church, some of their congregations did not enter the new Church. Sadly, church union always seems to leave behind some 'separated brethren' who do not wish to go that way.

I should not ignore the political situation in the 70s. In 1978, while I was attending a residential meeting of the Church Life Department Committee, the news came through that Mrs. Margaret Thatcher had been elected to the leadership of the Conservative Party. The then chairman of our departmental committee, the Revd Kenneth Slack, in a characteristically opinionated statement, ventured to say that this would ensure that the Labour Party would remain in power for at least the next decade. How wrong he proved to be! The Conservatives won the General Election in 1979 and Mrs. Thatcher was in power until her party ditched her in 1990: thus becoming the longest serving Prime Minister of the 20th Century. Her 'reign', for that is what it was in all but name, was characterised by an emphasis on individual responsibility. She is remembered for having curbed the power and influence of the Trades Unions and for dismantling the British coal industry, to name but two of her exploits. She might also be remembered for having dominated both her own party and others - 'the Iron Lady' as she became known – and for her infamous remark when addressing the General Assembly of the Church of Scotland, stating that 'there is no such thing as Society', a remark for which she was strongly and publicly upbraided by the then Moderator of that Assembly. Her policies have, however, influenced the political and common life of our country ever since, for good or for ill, during both Conservative and Labour administrations. She will certainly be remembered beyond her own generation – whether with admiration or loathing remains to be seen.

Our family, of course, were rapidly growing up during this period. Stephen and Rebekah were teenagers and becoming steadily more independent. Most of our holidays now did not include them, by their own choice. On several occasions we took Christopher and Judith to the Lake District, making use of a cottage owned in Keswick by John Neal, Frances's boss. We quite fell in love with this part of the world. The enjoyment, however, evaporated somewhat immediately when we returned home to find the house in turmoil and the sink full of dirty pots. 'We thought you were coming home tomorrow' was the usual comment!

The appointment as Secretary for Christian Education and Children's Work was termed for five years, though it was renewable. In 1979 I led a Church Weekend for the church in Palmers Green, North London. It was a stimulating experience, and when I got home I said to Frances: 'If ever I were looking for a church in North London, which I hope I never will be, Palmers Green would be about the only one I would consider'. At that time this was a purely hypothetical question, as they had a minister, the Revd James Dey. In 1980, however, he left to return to his native Scotland. Frances and I remembered our previous conversation. I asked her what I should do. 'Do nothing' she wisely said; 'if it is to be, they will come looking for you'. Imagine my astonishment, therefore, to arrive home one evening from an Elders' Meeting at Borehamwood nearby, where I was currently Interim Moderator, to hear that Michael Davies, who had become our Synod Moderator, had called in my absence and told her that Palmers Green had asked if I could be approached to consider becoming their minister! Yet once again an approach had come 'out of the blue'. Almost inevitably the process, which swung into action, led to a Call addressed to me early in 1981 – not quite unanimous, but strong enough to merit serious consideration. At the same time I had been invited to undertake a second term in the Christian Education post, but the urge to return to local pastoral ministry was strong, I accepted the Call from Palmers Green, and we prepared to move – yet again!

Chapter 12
THE MIDDLE YEARS – 1981-1992

I have never been more sure of the rightness of any move than when I accepted the Call to Palmers Green. I remember being in the vestry there on my first Sunday morning, and saying to David Jenkins, then the Church Secretary, that he had no idea how good it felt to have a congregation of my 'own' again. No longer would I be an itinerant preacher on Sundays. No longer would I move from one group of people to another in the pursuit of various projects. No longer would I feel detached from the local scene where the action has to be. I was coming 'home'. And throughout my eleven years as minister in Palmers Green neither Frances nor I felt any differently about it. I suppose many ministers, looking back on their ministries, feel that one pastorate was their most fulfilling one. In my case, though I was happy in all my pastorates, I would have no hesitation in saying that Palmers Green was the one for me.

I have told the story of this chapter in the life of Palmers Green Church in some detail in a book I wrote in 1997 entitled "Palmers' Progress". There are still some copies of that book on my shelves: they are available to anyone who would like to supplement what I am about to write here. I wrote it because, as I said in the preface, I felt that, while a good deal had been written and discussed about Christian mission in the inner city, in the city centre and in the countryside, very little study had been done of mission in suburbia. Yet it was here that the strongest congregations were situated upon whom mission in those other places was partly dependent. At the financial level alone, if churches like that in Palmers Green did not exist and contribute towards the support of work being done in the inner cities and the country towns and villages, those smaller churches would have no ministry. But it is true in other respects too. Quite properly the strong help the weak, while those who are apparently weak have something to give to those who are stronger from their very vulnerability. But this is not always openly acknowledged. There were times when I was at Palmers Green when I felt that the other churches in the District had something of a love-hate relationship with us: they knew they depended on us for leadership and support, but they envied our apparent success and sometimes seemed to feel themselves almost judged by it. It was a situation we found very difficult to resolve. So it was that my book was designed both to recount the story of eleven significant years in the life and development of a suburban church and to make a modest contribution to missiological thinking.

In 1870 Palmers Green was a tiny hamlet in the Middlesex countryside, surrounded by the estates of landed gentry. Around it Victorian suburbs were encroaching, but as yet they had not impinged upon its idyllic life. Then came the railway, the Hertford branch of the Great Northern Railway out of Kings Cross. At that time the GNR did not offer cheap workmen's tickets as did its competitor, the Great Eastern, so the housing that developed at Palmers Green was more commodious and expensive, attracting the middle classes, than that which developed in places like Tottenham and Edmonton to the east. Most of modern Palmers Green was built in the early part of the 20th century and between the wars. Now, many of the larger villas in the heart of the district have been turned into flats and the area is populated by an increasing number of young executives on their way up the social ladder, together with many people of Cypriot origin, moving out from their former stronghold in Stoke Newington. There are, however, still many houses occupied by families and some by older retired people who have lived there for most of their lives. 'Palmer' was another name for a pilgrim, a person on a journey, and there was a sense in which Palmers Green felt as if it too was 'on the way'. It is situated half way around the North Circular Road and half way between the city centre and the Hertfordshire countryside; and its population is constantly changing – a mingling of transitoriness and stability. We often said that if one had to live in London, Palmers Green was as good a place as any in which to live.

The church to which I was called in 1981 was itself in a state of transition. In 1975, three years after the United Reformed Church came into being, there were two congregations, one formerly Presbyterian and one formerly Congregationalist, in the same street, no more than 400 yards apart. When the ministers of both moved away, the District Council declared one ministerial vacancy, on the understanding that the two churches would unite under the minister who was called. To add to the complication of the situation, the Church at St James-at-Bowes, a mile or two away in Bounds Green, itself a union of Congregationalists and Presbyterians from 1947 but now much reduced in numbers, was drawn into the negotiations in 1976. The process of uniting was not easy, not least because of the difficulty of deciding which building to use. Both were suitable, but both had drawbacks. After a protracted struggle, and having eventually agreed to accept the advice of an outside arbiter, the decision has been made in 1979. The church was now worshipping in the former Congregational building, and the former Presbyterian building had been sold, demolished and replaced by a somewhat unsightly block of flats. The scars of the battle, however, remained. A number of members of both congregations had left or were sitting on the fringes of the life of the church. Some had become disillusioned by what the tensions of uniting had revealed about the unsatisfactory way in which Christians under pressure sometimes behave to one another. On Sundays, the former 'Congoes' sat on one side of the central aisle and the former 'Presbys' sat on the other side! Yet at the heart of the life of the church was a strong body of elders, most of whom saw both the vision and the necessity of the union that had taken place and were determined to make it work. It was these leaders who attracted me to the place. When I was considering the Call, the former General Secretary of the United Reformed Church, the Revd Arthur Macarthur, said that Palmers Green was the kind of place where the United Reformed Church needed to work and to succeed. I saw this as a challenge I was prepared to face.

We quickly settled in to the manse in Cranley Gardens – an end-of-terrace Edwardian villa with five bedrooms and large living rooms. Coincidentally, it had once been the home of a minister of St James-at-Bowes Church, a fact that pleased the members who had come from that church. It had a warm, friendly atmosphere. At first Rebekah, not pleased about the family moving yet again, remained with friends in Mill Hill, coming to live with us later. Christopher settled well into the Minchenden Secondary School. We discovered after we had moved that he had been bullied at the school in Mill Hill and was glad to move. For a year we took Judith back to Mill Hill daily so that she could finish her junior schooling there before entering Minchenden a year later. Thus, of all our children, Judith was able, despite our many moves, to complete her schooling without interruption at all three levels, infant, junior and secondary.

Frances continued for some years to work for John Neal in Hendon, though the family firm had been taken over by the giant Bairstow-Eaves. This entailed working in a number of different locations and after a while she started to look elsewhere for employment. Knowing this, our friend Clem Frank offered her a vacancy in the Finance Department at United Reformed Church House. Thus from 1986 until we moved away from London in 1992, she commuted from

Palmers Green station three days a week to work in the Maintenance of the Ministry office, responsible for ensuring that the contributions to that central fund from the local churches came in and were dealt with appropriately. She was very happy working in that office, partly because her colleagues were very pleasant company, and partly because she came to know many ministers and church treasurers across the country, if only by phone. Her immediate colleague was Judy Stockings. Judy has worked in the Finance Office of the United Reformed Church since 1977 and is known, even loved, by every minister in the Church. She treats everyone the same and has time for everyone, even those who phone with the most trivial problems. She and Frances sat opposite one another in the office, and Clem loves to tell how (being women, of course!) they were able to talk to one another about different subjects simultaneously, and also get on with their work, all at the same time!

The congregation at Palmers Green declared itself to have 374 members in 1981. The church secretary reckoned that the realistic active membership was about 200, and so it proved to be. In addition we had about 50 children. Interestingly, when we came to leave in 1992 the church had 201 members, thus showing that we had maintained our total effective membership across the eleven years. More interesting still, however, was the fact that of the 200 who were there in 1992, about 100 had been received into membership during the time I had been minister there, an indication of the constant movement in a suburban congregation which can be both a weakness and a strength.

The age profile of the Palmers Green congregation was on the high side, but we also attracted a number of young families and an interesting and significant group of single young adults. My predecessor had had the knack of spotting talent and harnessing it for the worship of the church. We followed the trail he had forged and developed a pattern of having an occasional Sunday morning service prepared and carried through by a number of church members under my leadership, and a monthly Sunday evening service known as 'Second Sunday evening' when, once again, a group of members would be responsible with me for the service. This enabled all kinds of innovation to take place. Drama, dance, music, visual art were all employed to enable a theme to become a corporate act of worship. I never cease to be grateful for the immense amount of talent that emerged in that congregation, or for the fact that people were prepared to put their gifts at the disposal of the church. I used sometimes to say that, whereas in previous pastorates people had usually followed the lead that I sought to give, in Palmers Green I spent a lot of my time frantically trying to catch up with many of the members of the congregation!

But this was not all. The same talents were harnessed to produce a number of unique musical productions, the music being written either by Paul Bateman or John Strange, two of our regular organists, and the words usually by Fredwyn Hosier or sometimes by Jill Jenkins. Titles I remember are 'Pilgrim's Progress' (which happened a year or two before I arrived), 'The Knights of the Square Table', 'The Prodigal Son', 'The Good Samaritan', 'Gift and Sign', 'Alice Through the Looking Glass', 'Winnie the Pooh', 'Bumble Bee 1 and 2'. Paul Bateman also wrote a Rock Mass which we performed as an act of worship on at least one occasion, and 'Bethlehem Blues', music for words written by the Revd Stuart Jackman. There were others, both sacred and secular, all home-grown productions which both enhanced the sense of fellowship in the church and made an impact upon the community around. These musical productions did a great deal to draw together those who had formerly been members of the different churches which combined to create Palmers Green United Reformed Church in 1975/6.

We had not been in Palmers Green for more than a year when the then Prime Minister, Margaret Thatcher, took the country into war with Argentina in the Falkland Islands. The controversy over this policy reminded me of that which had divided the country at the time of the Suez crisis and the Russian invasion of Hungary in 1956, only this time only the UK were directly involved. It was not a pretty sight to see our service men and women flying and sailing off to the other side of the world to defend a small group of islands that were one of the last vestiges of the British Empire. When the war was over, a thanksgiving service was held in St Paul's Cathedral and I remember Mrs. Thatcher's public anger that the then Archbishop of Canterbury, Dr Robert Runcie, included in the service prayers for the Argentines as well as for our own country. To most of us this seemed perfectly natural. If ever there was a war that might be said to have been justifiable, and that achieved what it set out to achieve, I suppose this was it. I was, however, and remain, highly perturbed that our nation chose to settle its differences with another nation in this way.

During the 1980s the United Reformed Church instituted a programme of sabbatical leave for ministers. We became entitled to three months away from the pastorate every ten years, with a limited amount of funding for study and research. I had my first experience of such leave in the Spring of 1984. As we were beginning as a church to look outwards towards the community, I chose to undertake some study in missiology at Selly Oak in Birmingham and to intersperse this with visits to churches around the country that were known to be addressing the needs of their community in positive and adventurous ways – affecting both their congregational attitudes and the use of their buildings. The period of leave passed all too quickly, but the insights I gained undoubtedly paid off in the way the life of the church developed over the next few years.

The direction of the church's mission had, however, already been set. In 1982 I was encouraged by the elders to visit the Social Services Department of the Enfield Borough Council to discuss the needs of our community. There I was told that there was an urgent need to find ways of supporting the many elderly housebound people who lived in the area, often in flats that had been constructed in the houses where they had once brought up their families, but were now living alone and somewhat isolated. With the help of the Department we set up what became known as the 'Burford Day Centre', providing transport to bring the guests to the church rooms and offering a programme of social interaction and a hot lunch on one day, later two days, a week. That Day Centre has now been operating for 26 years and has rarely ceased to have a full complement of guests, chosen from referrals by the Social Services and other agencies. For many years we owed a great deal, in this and in many other ways, to the dedicated enthusiasm of Cecilia Whiting, one of our elders, who was appointed leader of the Centre, and her husband Ron. The centre is still staffed entirely by volunteers, members of the church and others, and thus is able to keep its costs to a minimum. It has proved to be literally a life-saver for many frail elderly people. Equally importantly, in its early days it enlisted the help of people from all three former churches within the congregation, and proved to be a vital unifying factor in the process of integration. When a church looks outwards and involves itself in mission it discovers a deep unity of relationship and purpose.

From this Day Centre we developed short acts of weekday worship. 'This is a church, isn't it?' said some of the guests, 'so why can't we have a service?' Thus it was that at noon on Wednesdays and Thursdays (the days the Day Centre was in operation), in a small side chapel, fifteen minutes of informal worship took place, led sometimes by me and more often by members of the church. A real need among some of the otherwise house-bound elderly people for worship was thus met. In time, without any pressure, a few of these became members of the church.

As an indirect consequence of the establishment of the Day Centre I became involved with Age Concern. It began with an application for funding but led to the development of relationships with the area staff. They badly wanted to establish a branch in the borough of Enfield where we were situated but were looking for leadership. To cut a long story short, after a spell serving on the committee, I became Chairman of the newly established Age Concern Enfield, an involvement which I found very interesting and, I felt, a suitable extension of my ministry. In time Age Concern also set up a Day Centre, using our premises for a while before moving to more suitable accommodation elsewhere.

Our outward-looking attitude developed in other directions too. The premises became known as 'The Burford Centre' – Burford Gardens being the road at the side of the church. This Centre was designed to serve the needs of the community around. Already Scouts, Guides, a Play-Group and other regular community activities took place there. Later a drama group called 'Chicken-Shed', catering for physically challenged and able-bodied youngsters, held their activities there for a good many years. But community service sponsored by the church itself, together with other local churches, also began during those years. We formed an ecumenical Amnesty Group to give support to political prisoners. And we set up, again with the support of other churches, an Access and Child Contact Centre where separated parents, especially those prevented by the courts from having unsupervised access, could come and meet their children on a regular basis. We thus demonstrated that we wanted to be a 'community to enhance community' – a phrase we often used to make our aims clear to ourselves and to others.

With my ecumenical zeal I was anxious to play my part in the inter-church activity of the neighbourhood. The Palmers Green Council of Churches, I discovered, comprised five congregations: Methodist, Roman Catholic, Anglican, Baptist and ourselves. This seemed to me to offer the ideal mix - all the main-stream Churches of the country were represented, but no one denomination outnumbered the others or was tempted to dominate. At the core of the organisation was a strong and lively ministers' meeting, whereby as colleagues we got to know each other well. This was the era of 'the Local Ecumenical Project', a scheme of the then British Council of Churches to encourage local churches to integrate their worship, work and witness. One version of these 'LEPs', as they came to be known, was for congregations of different denominations to sign a covenant between them to work together as much as possible and not to do apart what could more appropriately be done together. It seemed to me that Palmers Green was potentially fruitful soil for such a relationship and when I became Chairman of the Council of Churches I took steps to bring it about. In September 1987 a covenant was signed between the Anglican, Methodist, Roman Catholic and United Reformed Churches at a memorable service in the Anglican church and we became known as 'The Uniting Churches of Palmers Green'. The Baptist Church did not come with us at the time, but a few years later became involved. A week or two before the day when our covenant was signed an historic conference had taken place at Swanwick in Derbyshire which declared that the participating Churches (including the Romans Catholics, who had not been part of the British Council of Churches) were now 'pilgrims together' on the road to unity. This brought into being Churches Together in Britain and Ireland. Our covenant was thus the first to be established following this Swanwick conference. Over the years since 1987 the relationship has sometimes strengthened, sometimes weakened, heavily dependent upon the commitment of the clergy and ministers who have been in post, but it survives to this day and makes its local witness to the unifying power of God's Spirit among God's people.

The Greater London boroughs operated a system of Borough Deans, whereby each denomination who wished to do so nominated one of their number to represent them on an ecumenical group, principally to relate to the Borough Council and its chief officers. In due time I was asked by the Moderator of our Synod to become the United Reformed Church's Borough Dean for Enfield and enjoyed this further extension to my ministry in the area.

I was also serving my own denomination more widely than through the local church. Early on in my time in Palmers Green I was elected President of what became the Lea Valley District Council and later served as the Convener of its Pastoral Committee for several years. I was also a member of the Synod Executive Council and later became its Chairman. Some of us at Palmers Green Church had a large part in arranging and carrying through District and Synod Days and weekend conferences at the High Leigh Conference Centre in Hertfordshire.

Additionally, we held a number of Church Weekends for our own congregation, sometimes at High Leigh, sometimes at a Roman Catholic retreat centre at London Colney, and sometimes on our home territory, as well as weekends away for the young people of our church, sleeping on church hall floors. We also developed a series of Church Holidays in places as far-flung as North Devon, West Wales, South West Scotland and Gloucestershire. This was indeed an active ministry in an active Church!

In 1986 we broadcast a Sunday service on Radio 4. In those days this service was put on air, live, at 9.30 in the morning. We were told that over one million people listened. Being a church that attempted to operate as an all-age community, we decided to offer an act of worship, prepared by a group of members, in which over a dozen people of all ages took part. From the mail we received subsequently our experiment appeared to have been widely appreciated – though I am not aware of it having been attempted anywhere else since! My on-air profile has not been particularly significant over the years. Later, while in Manchester, I was called in from time to time to give a Christian viewpoint on the news, particularly early on Sunday mornings. Then, very recently, I have been involved with BBC Wales in their Sunday morning programme 'Celebration'. In 1996 I appeared briefly on BBC and ITV news bulletins, as I will describe in a later chapter. These brief opportunities have shown me how important it is to make the best use of the air-waves to present the Gospel – and how vital it is to maintain the witness of the Church locally so that there can be a base from which such activity can spring.

October 16 1987 was the night of the 'Great Storm'. A hurricane had been approaching northern France, but Michael Fish the BBC weather forecaster confidently expressed the opinion the previous evening that it would not trouble the UK. Not so! In the early hours it struck southern England. We woke next morning completely cut off: no power, no telephone. Large trees, still in leaf and therefore fair game to the terrifying wind, were uprooted right across the country, Palmers Green included. There was an eerie silence everywhere. I had to travel that evening to an Assembly of the National Christian Education Council which I was chairing in Derbyshire. I got there, but most of the delegates did not. We were at the mercy of the weather than night – a sobering reminder of the power of nature to dominate human life.

The church building at Palmers Green, the former Congregational church, was large and impressive. Inside it was fitted out with oak pews and panelling: all very beautiful, but increasingly restrictive to the kind of participatory worship we were developing. I had cherished the possibility of re-ordering it, but bided my time and waited for the congregation to be ready for such a move and for a source of money to appear. This happened in 1987 when a former Presbyterian member, Nina Anderson, died and left approximately £70,000 to the church 'for the enhancement of its worship'. After much thought and prayer, and a good deal of discussion, plans were drawn up to strip the building of all its furniture, to level and carpet the floor, to replace the pews with chairs and to lower the pulpit and put it on casters to enable it to be moved around. 'Exchange of pulpits' would thus become a possibility in a way that was not envisaged when that term was coined! Other features included erecting a moveable screen two thirds of the way back, building coffee-making facilities in the rear area thus created, providing toilets near the entrance and positioning a screen across the apse to conceal the organ console: the only immovable piece of furniture. To ensure that the building would give the impression of always being open to the world, the oak entrance doors were fixed in an open position, turning outwards, and clear glass doors inserted into the open space. Our architect was Brian Smith, a long-standing member of the church. A nice feature was that the chairs for the congregation were made for us out of the wood of the pews by the brother of Brian Hosier, our then church secretary, and he also made a new octagonal communion table from the panelling that had formerly graced the walls of the apse. Thus we were using the materials already available within the building and acting responsibly from an environmental point of view. When finished, and set out for worship, with the chairs in semi-circles, the pulpit centrally at the front, and the communion table at the focal point of the semi-circle, we found we had, in effect, created a modern version of a 17th Century meeting house within a rectangular Edwardian church. It gladdened my heart one day when a visitor told me what a lovely building it was: 'light, open, warm and friendly, just like the congregation that worships here'. The building was re-dedicated at a special service in May 1990.

A pleasing feature of the eleven years I spent as minister in Palmers Green was the fact that no less than five members of the church entered the ministry of Word and Sacraments and one – Gillian Whiting – went as a missionary-teacher with the Council for World Mission to the Solomon Islands. Those entering the ministry were David Whiting, who has served in Furness, Sunderland, and Leeds and, now, as Industrial Chaplain on Teeside; David Miller, who has been minister in Peterborough for the past ten years; David Jenkins, formerly our church secretary, who was ordained to the non-stipendiary ministry locally; Janet Lees, who has ministered in Twickenham and Leeds; and Liz Brown who was ordained in our own church, first to return to Taiwan where she had formerly served as a missionary, then to serve as university chaplain in Leeds. A sixth church member also candidated and was accepted but withdrew from training part way through the course. It is, I imagine, always a source of satisfaction to a minister when a member of the church enters the ministry and one realises that one has had some share in that development.

In 1985 we celebrated our Silver Wedding and the 25th anniversary of my Ordination. The church, without our knowledge or approval, turned the Harvest Supper that year into a celebration of both events and presented us with a beautiful hand-made fruit bowl, a lovely preaching stole for me made by two of the members, and a cheque which they specifically said we were to use for 'something frivolous'. We used it to finance a pleasant weekend in a luxury hotel in Banbury, Oxfordshire. The family organised a surprise party in our own home, having got us out of the house by a cunning ruse in order to prepare for it. They had invited many of the church members and some of our friends from all over the country. It was a lovely evening, made very special by the knowledge that they had wanted to do it and had arranged it so carefully and successfully. The only thing we ourselves had planned to do was to spend a long weekend in Paris, which we also very much enjoyed.

Without doubt the most memorable task that came to me during my time at Palmers Green came, like every other opportunity, quite unsought. In 1988 I was nominated by my own Church Meeting, and then by my Provincial Synod, to become Moderator of the United Reformed Church's General Assembly for the year 1989-90, and was duly elected from among six such candidates at the Assembly meeting in Southport. This form of leadership is a rare privilege and, by its very nature, comes to comparatively few people and rarely to a minister in pastoral charge of a congregation. I was suitably humbled, however, when speaking with the local Roman Catholic assistant priest who had telephoned to congratulate me. 'It is the highest honour my Church can bestow', I said in my arrogance. 'No', came the immediate response, 'it is the highest form of service you can be called upon to perform'. I hope I carried out the tasks in that spirit.

The only prescribed task expected of the Moderator is to chair the sessions of the General Assembly and its Executive Committee. Beyond that, it is very much a representative role. General Assembly Moderators travel the country, fulfilling preaching and speaking engagements, attending ceremonial events, visiting the Assemblies of other Churches and some of the Synods and District Councils of their own Church. They are also expected to undertake two overseas tours, one to a Reformed Church in a European country and one to a Church in a country with whom the United Reformed Church is linked through the Council for World Mission.

The year began with an induction, not, as is usually the case, at the General Assembly itself, but in my own church at Palmers Green. This was because, for the first time, the dates of the Assembly were being changed from May to July and it was thought advisable that I should begin my year of office in May. I found it reassuring to be inducted in the presence of my own congregation, and thus to be physically reminded of the support I knew they would give. They symbolised their support in the following weeks and months by displaying a map at the back of the church and plotting on it, week by week, where we would be.

With Archbishop Runcie 1990 during years as moderator of General Assembly

For our link visit to a country with whom the United Reformed Church is linked through the Council for World Mission it had been arranged for us to visit South Africa. As it turned out, fortuitously we were there at a very significant time in the history of that country. We visited the Assemblies of the Presbyterian Church and the United Congregational Church of Southern Africa and were very warmly received. Addressing the Presbyterian Assembly I mentioned the support the Churches in the UK had tried to give to South African Churches during the Apartheid regime, not least through our affirmation of the strict sanctions our government had imposed. To my surprise this evoked a standing ovation – the only one I have ever received in my life! It was noticeable, however, that there were some white 'boer' members of the Assembly who did not take part in this demonstration, and when the session was over I was taken aside by them and told in no uncertain manner that what I had said was not acceptable. So be it; but this was 1989, and Frances and I were in their country when the last segregated election took place, returning FW DeClerk to power. Immediately afterwards he lifted the state of emergency and we witnessed huge demonstrations of freedom in Durban, Johannesburg and Capetown. In the following February Nelson Mandela was released from jail and the whole Apartheid system crumbled before the astonished gaze of the world. I have often wondered how those burly white Presbyterians have coped with the radical change that has taken place since then.

Our European visit was to the Evangelical Church of the Czech Brethren. We went there at Easter 1990 – just a few months after their 'velvet revolution' had released the country from Russian domination. It was a rare privilege to be asked to preach in Prague on the first Easter Day after this revolution had taken place. It was a moving experience to serve communion in that service to eager worshippers who came forward to receive the bread and wine, in some cases with tears in their eyes. This was fellowship at a deep level. Services of Holy Communion have rarely meant more to me than that one that Easter in Prague. While in Czechoslovakia, as in South Africa, we met many church leaders who had carried the Church through the years of oppression and we were astonished at their resilience and courage, and the way they had kept faith and hope alive during all that time. We were also amazed that, after such a long subjugation to the Communist regime, they were sloughing it off so easily and confidently. I am told that the Czech republic has become thoroughly westernised since then, for good and for ill.

For good measure, in the November of 1989, I was asked to go to East Berlin to greet the leaders of the Evangelical Church of the Union just a day or two after the wall between East and West Germany had been breached. Berlin was alive with an electric atmosphere. At the Freidrichstrasse rail station I joined the queues of East Berliners crowding to visit the west, in some cases for the first time in their lives. I was conducted around the city by Frau Grengel, a pastor of the Church whose offices I was visiting. She shared a personal story with me. When the Iron Curtain had come crashing down across Berlin she had been engaged to be married to a West German pastor. They were forced to go their separate ways. But on the day previous to my visit they had met again at one of the now open crossing points. He had married in the meantime and raised a family; she had never married; but the meeting had understandably been poignant in the extreme: just one story of millions that could be told from that time. Once again, it was a rare privilege to be there in a year packed with privilege. My period of office proved to be a unique one in terms of international developments and opportunities.

One of the saddest visits I paid was to the General Assembly of the Presbyterian Church of Ireland of Belfast – sad because of the divisions it revealed in both Church and nation. As I arrived Ian Paisley and his Free Presbyterians were demonstrating outside the assembly building, protesting against the fact that the Assembly was to debate the matter of membership of the proposed Churches Together in Britain and Ireland, the new body in which the Roman Catholic Church was to be a full member. When the debate itself took place some days later there was visible and palpable acrimony on the Assembly floor, stirred up by members who had been bussed in specially for the debate. The vote, when it was taken, was against membership of the new body – whereupon scores of ecumenically minded representatives queued up to register their dissent from the decision. The ecclesiastical and political divisions in the province were revealed both in assembly debates and in the streets around, where armed soldiers were to be seen at every corner. It is little short of a miracle, and a matter for great rejoicing, that, seventeen years later, as I write, peace appears to have come to Northern Ireland with Ian Paisley as First Minister and Martin McGuiness as deputy in the province's Assembly. Our visit to the Church of Scotland Assembly, by contrast, was an uplifting and, in parts, inspiring experience.

Representing the Church to the nation during my year of office entailed three memorable events. First, it was customary then for the Moderator to host a tea party at the Houses of Parliament for members of both houses who had a declared personal connection with the United Reformed Church. It was good on that occasion to chat informally with Lord Harold Wilson, Lord Michael Cocks (the son of my college principal), Sir Teddy Taylor, Nigel Spearing and others and to acknowledge their Christian commitment to the political process. An added bonus was to sit in the visitors' gallery of the House of Commons later that evening and to witness the emotion of the moment when it was announced that Nigel Lawson had resigned as Chancellor of the Exchequer.

The second national event the Moderator is expected to attend is the Remembrance Day ceremony at the Cenotaph in Whitehall. I found this occasion very moving. It was also an experience to be robing in the room where Prime Ministers past and present were assembling. I cherish the memory of being in conversation with Harold Wilson when Ted Heath entered the room. "Oh there's Ted," he said. "I haven't spoken to him for years and I have no intention of changing my mind now!"

The third national event, if we may call it that, was to be invited to attend the Houses of Parliament Prayer Breakfast. It was a large and lavish affair, taking place in the Queen Elizabeth Conference Centre in Westminster. The speaker at this breakfast was the Revd John Stott, an Anglican priest of an evangelical persuasion whom I have always much admired. It was something of a surprise for us to be seated at a table with the Speaker of the House of Commons, Bernard Weatherall, the Secretary General of the Commonwealth, the British Ambassador to the Holy See, the head of the Metropolitan Police – and the Prime Minister, Margaret Thatcher. Snatches of the conversation come to mind still and, among other impressions, remind me that all these people are human beings! The event took place a few days after the terrible Tiananmen Square Massacre in Peking. Commenting, Mrs. Thatcher said: 'That's the way to do it : get as many protesters out on the square as you can find; they wouldn't be able to shoot them all; they wouldn't have enough bullets!' We wondered whether this was the level at which our foreign policy was conducted at that time.

A rare privilege for the Moderator is to be invited to a Garden Party at Buckingham Palace. The invitation, according to royal etiquette, came to Mrs. Forecast, for her 'husband and unmarried daughters'. Judith was delighted to come with us, and was probably the only young woman who has ever attended such an event in an Oxfam dress and plimsoles! It was a hot, sunny day, and we greatly enjoyed the event – even if the ice-cream melted in the heat! We were not among those who were invited to be introduced to the Queen, but were glad to have had the experience.

Ecumenical engagements came thick and fast. It was somewhat daunting to be present at such gatherings, especially when people would turn to me and say: 'What does the United Reformed Church think, or say, or do, about this, that or the other matter.' One event stands out in my memory. I was asked to preside at an ecumenical eucharist in our little church in Bromley-by-Bow in east London. Participants were gathered in a large circle for the communion. As I broke the bread and handed a piece to my neighbour on my left I realised that this was the Anglican Bishop of Stepney, Jim Thompson, graciously and perfectly naturally receiving the sacrament from a United Reformed Church minister. Into my mind there and then there flashed a memory of when I had been invited to preach at a eucharistic service in an Anglican church in Plymouth during the Week or Prayer for Christian Unity way back in 1968. In welcoming me the parish priest had said publicly and unapologetically that 'of course Mr Forecast will not be permitted to share with us in communion.' Despite what we sometimes believe to be the case, the barriers are gradually yielding

In addition to these responsibilities and opportunities, my year of office involved some one hundred and fifty local church visits and many miles of travelling. Frances was able to come with me for most of these visits, though in the autumn, just after we returned from South Africa, she entered hospital to have her gall bladder removed, at a time when this operation still involved major surgery. She recovered in time, however, to join me to visit the national youth event 'Connect' in Bristol a few weeks later.

In some ways the visits to local churches proved to be among the most interesting and encouraging experiences of the year. We were warmly welcomed, for the most part, by lively congregations doing exciting things in their work and witness and gained an overall impression of a Church that, despite the statistics of decline, was in good heart and motivated by a divine Spirit. Not long before we embarked on the year of office our Church in Palmers Green had received a 'Peace Candle' which had originated in a church in Russia. One of our elders suggested that I might take one to every congregation I visited as a sign of fellowship, peace and hope. This I did. There was one church in Lancashire where the minister said he had tried to introduce this feature only to be rebuffed by the congregation: yet here was I, all unknowing, coming in and doing the very thing he had failed to do! But in almost every place the gesture was greatly appreciated, and I am told that there are churches up and down the land where peace candles are lit in worship to this day.

There were times when the travelling proved to be a little exhausting. One Sunday I led worship in the morning in Goole in south Yorkshire and in the evening in Alnwick in Northumberland. The following morning, Frances opened one eye and asked, not 'What day is it?' but 'Where are we?'

The Moderator of General Assembly is not released from the pastorate or other work to which he or she is committed. I led worship at Palmers Green approximately once every six weeks, including over the Christmas period. I also continued with as many of my weekday responsibilities as possible. Additionally, the modifications we made to the interior of the church building happened during this year, ensuring that nearly always there was a meeting of the building committee to attend every time I was at home. So life was full and tiring, but also very stimulating.

I suppose the Moderator gets an untypical view of the life of the Church, as one tends to get invited to those places where good things are happening. But it is an immense privilege to visit those places, to affirm those good things, and to realise that even at a time when the institutional Church is declining there is much for which to give thanks. This year of office was indeed one of the most memorable experiences of my life, for which I shall always be more grateful than I can say. It was good, however, to come down to earth and to come home. The congregation had not noticeably suffered through my continued absence – perhaps, indeed, had gained from it! We were welcomed back with a mediaeval banquet such as only Palmers Green could stage. We had been fortunate, during my time away, that the church had had the services of no less that three ordained ministers: David Jenkins, who was linked with our church pastorally; Geoffrey Satchell, Thames North Province's Synod Clerk who, in semi-retirement, was a member of the church; and Terry Oakley, a officer on Church House staff who was also a church member with us. These three had given the oversight that was required in my absence, enabling me to pick up the threads easily and quickly.

While we were living in Palmers Green my parents and Frances's father died. My father died in January 1984 – the first of our family's four grandparents to do so. His health had been failing for some time but his passing, when it came, was a shock to us all. He was, nevertheless, 85 years old, he died at home having written suggestions for hymns and readings at his funeral service the night before, and there was a sense that his life, having been lived to the full, was now complete. I remember thinking, however, that with his death I was now 'head of the family' and that my generation was now the next in succession. Frances's father contracted Alzheimer's Disease and died in somewhat traumatic circumstances in hospital in Oxford in 1988 at the age of 77. This wretched disease had significantly changed his personality towards the end and it was a mercy when he died. For the last few days he sat is a corner and neither ate nor drank. It seems that he chose to go, and who could blame him? My mother maintained an independent life for ten years after my father died but passed away in hospital in Ipswich the Spring of 1992, having contracted a form of leukemia. She, like my father, was 85. She knew that we were soon to move to Manchester and that I was to become a Synod Moderator, but did not live to see it take place. She had, however, been present at my induction as Moderator of the General Assembly and had, I know, taken pride in all we did while I held that office. I know that she was particularly pleased that for preaching during that year I had used my father's gown as a symbol of my solidarity with him. Frances's mother lived on until 2002, having celebrated her 90th birthday. She died peacefully and without any fuss in her own home in Thame. Thus all those of that generation in the family have now died – and my contemporaries and I, who thought we were middle-aged, are now the senior members of our families and must appear elderly, if not old, to our own children and grandchildren!

In July 1991 my Aunt Muriel died. She was my mother's youngest sibling and lived in North Wales. During the war she had served as a cook in the Women's Auxiliary Air Force and later became cook at Penrhos College, a Methodist girls' boarding school in Colwyn Bay. In her late forties she married Austin Hulme, a widower who had lived in Queens Avenue, Old Colwyn since the house was built in 1935. I played the organ for their wedding, conducted by my father, in Stoke on Trent in 1963. Only nineteen years older than I, she had always been something of a favourite aunt. When she died, her husband having pre-deceased her, we discovered that she had left her house jointly to my cousin Keith Goulding and to me. Most generously, Keith declared that he had no need for the house and made the whole thing over to me. For the first time in our lives, therefore, we became home-owners. We resolved to keep the house, use it for holiday breaks, and make it available to family and friends for the same purpose. It proved to be a wonderful 'bolt-hole'. While we remained in London, from time to time I would pick Frances up from the station on

Wednesday tea-time, drive up to Old Colwyn, and stay there until Saturday afternoon. After we moved to Manchester in 1992 we used to plan a weekend a month there – a much more satisfactory arrangement, we found, than trying to take a day off a week, and often failing to do so. In addition, many people from the North West and other parts used it for holidays. We felt sure Auntie Muriel would have been pleased about this. This house was later to fulfil an even more prominent role in my life in a way I could not have foreseen when it became ours in 1991.

During our time in Palmers Green we began to take holidays abroad. In the winter of 1987/8 I contracted influenza three times. In April, unbeknown to me, Frances went into the travel agent and asked where we could go without too much expense for some warm sun to help me recover. She, Judith and I went to Tenerife for a week and enjoyed it greatly. Subsequently Frances and I travelled together to Malta, Tunisia, Austria, Madeira, Gran Canaria, and Lanzarote. While we were in Madeira we purchased a timeshare which has been used both there and, by transfer, in Portugal and Spain several times, first by Frances and me together and then, more recently, by myself, either alone or with Howard and Margaret Starr. It has proved to be a boon, even if not as cheap to own and maintain as those who sold it to us implied!

Early in 1991 I began to wonder whether my time at Palmers Green might be coming to an end. New things were still happening. There was no obvious reason for me to move, but I was now 56 and realised that, unless I were to stay in Palmers Green until I retired, I ought to be considering my future. I had never been in favour of very long ministries, believing as a rule of thumb that ten or eleven years was usually about as long as any ministry should last. I also believed that it was better, if possible, to move while one still had some ideas and good things were still happening, than to wait until everyone was longing for one to go! It was while I was thus thinking and praying that I was asked, in the autumn of 1991, to meet the group appointed to seek a new Moderator for the North Western Province of the United Reformed Church. The Revd Tony Burnham, who had served there for ten years, had been appointed General Secretary of the Church and thus was about to leave a vacancy. Yet once again, an approach had come quite unsought and I had to take it seriously. This was not the first time I had been asked to consider such a post. In 1985, when I had been in Palmers Green only four years I was asked to consider the Moderatorship of the Eastern Synod. The prospect was very inviting: my home territory would have been a very pleasant place to serve. But a conversation with a valued colleague showed me clearly that when what seems like the right job comes up at what is evidently the wrong time, it cannot be the right job, and with some pain I declined. In 1987 another such approach was made; would I consider becoming Moderator of the Mersey Synod, centring on Liverpool. But by now I was even more enmeshed in projects that seemed to require my presence in Palmers Green, so once again I declined. This time, though, it began to feel like the right time. I therefore visited Manchester for the all-important meeting with the appointing commission and was given a unanimous Call. Frances and I both felt that this was now the leading we were seeking, and so I accepted. We were not expected to move until the summer of 1992, but the die was cast. We knew little about Manchester, and what we knew did not greatly attract us. How wrong we were! Manchester and the North West of England proved to be yet another pleasant place for us.

The remainder of our time at Palmers Green passed all too swiftly. Our departure was marked by an evening event incorporating a lovely supper and a 'This is your Palmers Green life' presentation which we thoroughly enjoyed. We were presented with a substantial cheque (with which we later bought a modern keyboard to replace our aged piano), a table cloth on which were embroidered the names of everyone associated with the church, and a beautiful coffee table, made to match the communion table in the church with some of the same wood by the same craftsman. Thus we came away with literally a tangible piece of the church and as rich a symbol of the corporate life of the congregation as could possibly be conceived. We left part of ourselves behind in exchange but left our happiest pastorate on the crest of a wave of love.

Chapter 13
UP NORTH – 1992–2000

We have never found it easy to leave a pastorate, and leaving Palmers Green proved to be the most difficult departure of all. We had, after all, been there for eleven years – longer than in any of the places where we had lived since our marriage. We had felt at home there from the start and had made some deep friendships. The work of the church had been most fulfilling, we had been involved in many creative developments, and the neighbourhood and the manse had been a very pleasant place in which to live. Fortunately the children were now grown up and had all left home. Rebekah had moved to America following her divorce from Paul. Stephen was living in his own house in Walthamstow. Christopher had graduated from Brunel University and was living with others in a flat in Wandsworth. And Judith was in her final year at Newcastle University. They all understood our desire to move and supported us as we prepared to do so. But the severing of deep roots proved to be almost physically painful for Frances and myself. Our final weekend was highly memorable, with a meal and a presentation of 'This is your Palmers Green Life' on the Saturday and two highly charged services on the Sunday. I was particularly touched that the congregations of the other Churches of the Palmers Green Covenant joined our own congregation in the evening for a service of dismissal presided over by our Synod Moderator, the Revd Janet Sowerbutts. Thus came to an end the most stimulating and satisfying period of my ministry and of our married life.

The North Western Synod of the United Reformed Church then comprised 164 churches in Greater Manchester, Lancashire and southern Cumbria. These churches had 12,600 members and 8,700 children in total. I came to believe that I had the most attractive province in the Church! It was quite compact, with good communications, but yet contained a wide variety of situations: commercial Manchester, affluent North Cheshire, post-industrial North East Lancashire, the Fylde coast with brash Blackpool and select Lytham St Annes, the hills and dales of Lancashire and the beauty of the southern Lake District. Town and country, suburb and inner city were all represented.

126

'It's grim up north' said the words of a song presented to me by my friend David Cornick in preparation for my induction in Manchester. From the start we found this well-known southern attitude to anywhere north of Watford to be totally false. The people were warm hearted and welcoming from the start, tending to call a spade a spade (or occasionally something else!) but 'up-front', loyal and committed. Frances had spent her early years in Leek, Blackpool and Bolton, and so had some knowledge of the culture, but, though I had the early experience of life in the Potteries to which I referred in an earlier chapter, as a southerner I had wondered whether I would settle among these northerners. I need not have worried. A colleague once said that for Lancastrians there are 'southerners and bloody southerners'. I think he implied that I was in the former category!

The manse into which we moved was in Didsbury, a very pleasant suburb in south Manchester – itself a city pulsating with life. It was not centrally situated within the province, because it had been bought for my predecessor, the Revd Tony Burnham, who already lived and worked in Manchester before being appointed and wanted to continue to live within the city boundary on account of his children's education. There was a lot more of the province north of Manchester than there was to the south, and occasionally the volume of traffic around and through the city, when I needed to travel northwards, was frustrating. But the advantages outweighed the disadvantages. From the house it was possible within an hour to be at the top of the Snake Pass in Derbyshire, and within an hour and a half to be in the Lancashire hills, the Lake District and the North Wales coast.

Not now being in pastoral charge of a congregation once again, we needed to decide where to hold our church membership. For a few months I undertook no preaching engagements and we visited a number of churches in the area. It was going to be more important for Frances to find a church where she would feel at home than for me, as I knew I would be there only rarely once my preaching ministry started. On the other hand, the importance of a local base for me would be to find in it the support my ministry would require and a congregation where I could feel at home on the rare occasions when I would worship there and attend other gatherings. As a result of our search, early in the new year of 2001 we were received into membership in the church in Gatley, a couple of miles away but easily accessible. The Revd Stephen Brown was then minister there, making a success of his first pastorate, and we soon made good friendships with him and his family and with members of the congregation. Some of them proved to be very supportive indeed in the years to come, in circumstances we could not possibly have foreseen when we settled among them.

My induction service to this new ministry turned out to be a highly inspiring occasion. It took place in the great hall of the University of Manchester Institute of Science and Technology, there being no church building in the province believed to be large enough for the number who might come. In the event, even this hall was not large enough, and some had to listen outside. Over 70 people came from Palmers Green, including the young adults' singing group who sang an item in the service – the song that was then quite new, 'I the Lord of sea and sky'. The song was accompanied by a liturgical dance performed by three young ladies from the church in Burnley, coached by Fredwyn Hosier from Palmers Green, who had met them at a dance workshop she had led at the Windermere Training Centre. The service was presided over by a former Moderator of Assembly, Mr. Ray Heritage, deputising for the current moderator who was unable to come. The Revd Dr David Cornick, to whom I had acted as pastoral advisor when he was first ordained, and who was now on the staff at Westminster College, Cambridge, preached an impressive sermon. David later became principal of the college and, later still, General Secretary of the United Reformed Church. Following the sermon, my own statement, and the act of induction, the welcome of the Synod was symbolised by each District presenting me with a tangible symbol of its life. Lancaster District presented a shepherd's crook (prompting snide remarks about bishops' croziers!), North West Lancashire a tin of treacle from the mythical 'Sabden treacle mines', the Fylde a 'present from Blackpool', North West Manchester a book about 20th century Salford, North East Manchester a weaver's shuttle, South West Manchester a Cheshire cheese and a Manchester City pennant, and South East Manchester some souvenir material that had been produced to support the bid Manchester was then making for the 2000 Olympic Games. It was all good fun, and a mark of the warm hospitality that was being offered us.

All Synods have an administrative office from which the Moderator usually works and where committee meetings are held. The office for the North Western Synod was situated in Eccles, to the west of the city of Salford, built on to the back of Patricroft United Reformed Church. It is to the credit of those who were running the operation during the previous decade that when they felt it desirable to move from offices in the centre of Manchester they chose this less-than-affluent neighbourhood in which to settle themselves. The location was also well situated for people to get there, and from which the Synod staff and I could travel to outlying parts of the province. We were well served by our office staff: Joan Seed and, later, Hazel Wall as administrative secretaries, and Gill Oldham and, later, Sue Wilkinson as my personal assistants.

Synod Moderators are appointed, not by the Provincial Synod where their ministry is primarily exercised, but by the General Assembly, though the Synod has a major role in the appointment process. They are thus responsible to the Assembly both for the pastoral care of the churches and ministers within their Synod and also for leadership within the denomination nationally. Within the Synod the work ranges over a wide area and a hugely varied number of congregations. I discovered that the Moderator engages with those churches either at their very best or their very worst. He or she is often called upon to share in the 'high days' of a church's life: the induction of a minister, a church anniversary, the launching of a particular mission project. On the other hand, she or he is often called in where there is trouble: tension and loss of confidence between a minister and the congregation, conflict among the members, ministers needing urgent support, perhaps questioning their calling or even their faith, domestic problems in manses. I vividly recall one morning when there were three or four such problems on my desk before 9.30 a.m. and I was beginning to feel that the whole Church was collapsing. I remember physically lifting my head and looking out of the window over the horizon, and reminding myself that out there were the great majority of churches and ministers getting on with the job conscientiously and harmoniously and making a consistent witness to their calling.

Moderators find themselves taking a full part in the wider councils of the United Reformed Church. At the top of the list of priorities are the monthly Moderators' Meetings, usually in London, at which the business always includes not only discussion of relevant issues but also the introduction of ministers to pastorates that are seeking them – a matter that has to be undertaken with the greatest care and sensitivity. Moderators also share in the work of the Church at Assembly level, within the Mission Council (the central executive body) and as members of Assembly committees, sometimes chairing them, as well as giving leadership to the Church in other ways. For most of my time in the North West I acted as Convener of the Assembly Ministries Committee, involving a good deal of work in guiding and presenting policy. During my time that Committee was called upon to prepare and present a new Disciplinary Procedure for ministers and I found myself chairing a working party to bring this about – a piece of work I had not expected and didn't feel particularly competent to undertake, but fortunately we had expert legal advice. I also served for a time as a member of the personnel committee within the World Church and Mission area.

Within the province, a Moderator is called upon to represent the United Reformed Church in ecumenical affairs. Churches Together in England, following its inauguration in 1990, set up regional work at county level. Within each region there was a Council and also a Church Leaders' Meeting. In the North West there were three such regional councils: Greater Manchester, Lancashire and Cumbria. Some of my colleagues had five or six to whom to relate – the price a smaller denomination pays for the fact that its own regional set-up covers a wider geographical area that that of some other denominations. It was in these meeting that I worked as colleague to Anglican and Roman Catholic Bishops, Methodist Chairs of Districts, a Baptist Area Superintendent, and occasionally representatives of the Orthodox and Black-led Churches. The colleagueship was stimulating and extremely enjoyable.

Just as a minister in a local pastorate, in my judgment, while getting fully involved in the wider life of the Church, should always give priority to the leadership of worship and pastoral care, so, as a Moderator, I continued to make this my aim. Ministers, after all, are ordained to the 'Ministry of Word and Sacraments', and that is their primary function. In this respect Moderators are no different from other ministers – and, indeed, within our ecclesiology, they are not a different 'order' of ministry, to which they need to be specifically 'ordained', but ministers of word and sacrament who are discharging this particular function for the time being. The Bishops of the Anglican and Catholic churches have a different status. Yet, I recall an interesting conversation with the Rt. Revd Christopher Mayfield who was then Bishop of Manchester, about the work we did. We discovered that, from a practical point of view, we worked very similarly. I had no power (but, admittedly, a good deal of influence!) and had to work in and through the Synod over which I presided. He theoretically had a good deal of personal power vested in him by virtue of his ordination as a bishop, but chose to work with and through his diocesan Synod. Thus we were experiencing ecumenical convergence.

Personally, I have long felt that, when the United Reformed Church came into being in 1972, we should have taken the bull by the horns and called our moderators Bishops, making it quite clear that this did not involve ordination in the so-called apostolic succession, but rather demonstrated a particular function of ministry to which they were appointed – a ministry of leadership and oversight. There are, after all, in the world a number of Reformed Churches, the Church in Hungary being one example, who have bishops of a reformed kind, and John Calvin himself was not against bishops as such, rather against the way their ministry had come to be exercised within the Roman Catholic Church of his day. In 1972 this would not have been acceptable, particularly to the Presbyterians who had a deep-seated aversion, historically conditioned, to Bishops and everything to do with them. But the debate surrounding conciliar and personal oversight rumbles on.

During my time in the North West some exciting new ventures took place. One concerned the pastoral oversight of the churches and the ministers, a function the constitution of the United Reformed Church clearly accords to the District Council, working together with the Synod Moderator. I discovered that, hitherto, only one of the seven District Councils within the province had a Pastoral Committee. I was not prepared to carry out my pastoral ministry without what I saw to be an essential part of the structure. We therefore brought about a new constitution for the Synod and its District Councils which ensured that, whatever else a District did or did not do, it had a Pastoral Committee and a Strategy Committee. I became a member of all seven Pastoral Committees and worked with them, I believe to everyone's benefit and satisfaction. Over the years, I came to rely heavily on the Conveners of these Pastoral Committees for confidential conversation, and indeed regarded them, to all intents and purposes, as 'suffragan bishops'.

High in the Pennine area of the Lancaster District, in the beautiful village of Ravenstonedale, stood a historic chapel together with a rather fine manse. The idea was to renovate the manse and turn it into a place where a minister might welcome people living under stress for periods of relaxation and healing. We were fortunate to obtain the interest of a minister who was prepared to work without stipend for a time, act as pastor to the little congregation, and offer the kind of hospitality we were envisaging in the house. For six years the Revd Mary Cock (later Howe) headed up this project. Sadly, eventually it failed for a variety of reasons, but not before a number of ministers had profited from what it offered. In 2000 Mary left for a pastorate in Herefordshire where, sadly, she died in 2006 from a brain tumour.

In post-industrial east Manchester we sponsored a ministry designed to pastor several tiny congregations and also to work with the statutory authorities for the enhancement of the life of the community. The Revd Brian O'Neill has ministered there now for many years, his stipend coming from the Ministry and Mission Fund despite the fact that the local churches can contribute little towards it. Latterly Brian was supported by the Revd Jack McKelvey, who had retired from the principalship of the Northern Theological College and offered to work without stipend in the pastorate, thus complementing Brian's work in the community. Jack and Brian are still there.

In the town of Blackburn we had a number of churches, but there was also the 'Blackburn Ragged School', an undenominational venture founded in the 19th Century to serve a poor working class area. The life of this fellowship had evolved over the years into what virtually amounted to a local church. Its officers had come to see that it needed the support of one of the established denominations if it was to survive and develop. They tried the Anglicans, and then the Methodists, but for various reasons those Churches felt unable to take responsibility. When they tried the United Reformed Church they was welcomed, and in 1995 became recognised as one of our local churches under the lay-pastorate of Mr. Alan Barnes, who had been an elder of the United Reformed Church in Essex before coming to Blackburn. He continues to minister there and the church continues to thrive under his leadership.

Westhoughton is a small town in its own right, but also a part of the borough of Bolton in North West Manchester. We already had a church there, but in the mid 90s an ecumenical project started on a new housing estate (The Hoskers) and we became involved with the Methodists and the Anglicans. The congregation met in the new building of a Church of England School, and for its composition drew on the children of the school and their parents. An ecumenical congregation of about 40 adults and 36 children continues to meet there under ministry provided by the United Reformed Church, Methodists and Anglicans.

In the centre of Manchester, at the heart of the university campus, stands St Peter's House, the base for an ecumenical chaplaincy. On Sundays a mixed congregation gathers there for worship, and in 1994 it was formally recognised as a local church of the United Reformed Church, in partnership with Anglicans, Methodists and Baptists. There are currently about 50 members, of whom 13 are United

Reformed, and a number of children. It is a significant witness to the uniting power of Christ in what has become a very secular environment.

A particularly successful one-off venture took place on July 15 1995. Despite the risk of arranging an outdoor event on St Swithin's Day, we organised a Synod Day to take place in Heaton Park, the largest park in Greater Manchester. We hired a large marquee and several smaller ones and invited churches to contribute a stall or sideshow according to their talents and opportunities. United Reformed Church organisations, both national and provincial, were featured and a series of 'ring events' for general enjoyment were arranged at intervals throughout the day. The event began and ended with worship led by a large choir and a band. The whole thing took a great deal of organising and a large amount of good will, but upwards of 3,000 people came – justifying, we felt, the purpose of the day. Despite a sharp shower after lunch, and the donkeys for children's rides going to the Synod Office instead of the park, the day was pronounced a great success, and played its part in helping members of local churches to feel part of something greater than their local fellowship.

These are just some of the many new ventures and projects with which I became involved during my time as Moderator of the North Western Synod. It was a happy, fulfilling time, albeit with some frustrations. Soon after I undertook the work someone asked Frances how I was getting on. 'Well, she said, he's been pretending to be a moderator for a long time, so it's about time he did it for real!' On another occasion, when asked the same question, she is reported to have said: 'He's taken to it like a duck to water – sickening isn't it!' I can honestly say, unlike some of my colleagues, that I really did enjoy the work. Over the years, the meetings of Synod twice a year became, in a sense, my congregation. I led the worship. I preached. I presided over the deliberations, rather as I had presided over the Church Meetings in Bristol, Plymouth, Cardiff and Palmers Green. The Pastoral Committees of the District Councils became, in effect, the elders with whom I shared ministry. I was still a minister of Word and Sacrament, simply on a different scale. It was a privilege to serve in this way for eight years.

One of the features of life in the North Western Synod that soon became apparent was that almost all the ministers had trained in what was originally known as The Lancashire Independent College housed in impressive buildings in Whalley Range in Manchester, and not a few of them had grown up in Lancashire and had all their pastorates in the county. While this made for strength and solidarity it did not always foster a sense of belonging to the wider life of the denomination and sometimes appeared to those outside like something of a closed shop. Indeed, the ministers of the North West were sometimes referred to as 'the Lancashire Mafia'! Over the years I took pains to introduce to pastorates ministers with training and experience elsewhere, so that by the time I retired there was a much healthier mix – those from elsewhere began to appreciate, as I did myself, the delights of Lancashire and Cheshire, while the local people learned to appreciate the gifts offered by those who came in. All in all we were blessed with a fine team of ministers in the Synod.

Frances meanwhile, the children having grown up and left home, and she no longer being the wife of the minister of the church to which we belonged, carved out a life for herself. She became a Samaritan, and found this activity most fulfilling. A little later she applied, and was accepted, to be a Magistrate on the Manchester bench and, again, found the work most rewarding. Meanwhile, day to day, she worked part-time, first at the local Withington Hospital, and then in the finance office of Luther King House, the home for several Theological Colleges making up the Partnership for Theological Education. She was thus working again for the Church, as she had done in London, and enjoyed doing so immensely.

For many years, as will have been evident in what I have written, I have had a keen interest in Christian Education. Upon my arrival in Manchester a new opportunity emerged which enabled me to develop this interest in a new way. I was invited to become a Governor of Northern College – the successor to Lancashire Independent College, now housed at Luther King House in Manchester serving the United Reformed Church and the Congregational Federation. There have been many developments in the life of this college during the years in which I have been associated with it, and the Governing Body has changed to keep abreast of these changes. The college is now a member of three educational partnerships. First, there is the Partnership for Theological Education which embraces the other colleges within Luther King House: Baptist, Methodist, Unitarian and Ecumenical. Then there is the South North Western Training Partnership, which has come into being more recently and includes the Anglicans from thee dioceses as well as the Free Church colleges. Finally there is the partnership of what are now known as the United Reformed Church Resource Centres for Learning, within which Northern College works with the other two United Reformed Church colleges: Westminster

College, Cambridge and the Scottish College in Glasgow, to serve both ordained and lay ministries. It remains to be seen how this complicated arrangement will work out for all concerned. For much of the time I served as a governor the Principal was the Revd Dr David Peel, a fine philosopher and theologian. He has been succeeded in the last few years by the Revd Dr John Campbell, a minister to whom I acted as senior advisor when he was ordained in Hackney in 1982. He has had a remarkable influence for good on both the college and the Partnerships since his arrival in 2004. Sadly, for all kinds of reasons, the number of people seeking ordination training has steadily declined in recent years, causing concern in many places. But the college is alive and well and urgently seeking to diversify its programme to include those who are not specifically seeking ordination.

One of the pleasant features of the corporate work of the Synod Moderators was a study-visit paid every third year to another country with a kindred Church. In 1995 we and our spouses paid such a visit to Berlin and Eastern Germany. It was fascinating to me to see the changes in the city since I had been there six years previously when I was Moderator of General Assembly. Frances and I stayed for part of the time with a German pastor and his wife and I preached in his church while he translated what I said. It was a moving and enriching experience.

One Saturday in June 1996 we were attending the induction of Sister Maureen Farrell as County Ecumenical Officer at a church not far from Manchester city centre. In the middle of the service a huge explosion told us that something ominous had happened. We soon discovered that a large IRA bomb had been detonated next to Marks and Spencers. Amazingly, largely because of the efficiency of the Greater Manchester Police, no one had been killed, but the area had been devastated. The threat of terrorism was thus brought home to us in a vivid way. The following Saturday, due to the initiative of our Synod Clerk, the Revd Ruth Wollaston, an ecumenical service was held in the damaged cathedral. I was invited to preach at this service – and, incidentally, appeared for the first and last time on the national TV news. When we were arranging it we had no idea how many people would come, and there would be no Sunday between making the arrangements and the arrival of the service to announce it in the churches. We had therefore to rely on local media and word of mouth. In the event the cathedral was filled to overflowing. It taught me that, for all its apparent marginalisation, the community still looks to the Church at times like this, and the Church has to be there to minister when such opportunities occur.

Mention must be made of the General Election in 1997. The Conservative Government had been running out of steam for several years, mired in uncertainty and sleaze. John Major, as Prime Minister following Mrs. Thatcher's resignation, had been much too pleasant a personality to cope with the challenges of leadership. No one really expected the party to win the election of 1993, but they did, by a slender majority. In 1997 it was different. Frances and I were invited to watch the publication of the results with some neighbours in our street, none of whom, as it turned out, had voted Tory. The atmosphere as the results came in was electric. Tory seat after Tory seat fell. The real excitement of the night was when Michael Portillo, who had been our MP when we lived in London, the holder of a hitherto rock solid Conservative seat, was ousted by Stephen Twigg, the young Labour candidate. It was the electoral moment of the decade! We returned home in the early hours delighted that Labour had won the election by a landslide. Tony Blair became Prime Minister and held office for ten years, winning three elections. He began well, but sadly disappointed many people, some within his own party, for the personal style of government he exercised and the arrogance he displayed. In particular his involvement in the war and occupation of Iraq made him many enemies. In June 2007 he resigned and made way for Gordon Brown, formerly Chancellor of the Exchequer. As I write it remains to be seen whether the fortunes of the Government will improve under Mr Brown's leadership.

Soon after the excitement of the 1997 election our life in Manchester was deeply overshadowed by serious illness. In May Frances was diagnosed with breast cancer. It turned out that she had probably had it for about five years, but it had not shown up on any of the regular mammograms to which she had been subjected. It was not until she had a minor fall that tiny shards of cancer coalesced into a large tumour in her right breast. Throughout the process of treatment, which extended over 14 months altogether, she was amazingly positive and serene. We were fortunate to live within a quarter of a mile of one of the best cancer hospitals in Britain: the Christie Hospital in Withington. The chemotherapy, which proved to be quite distressing in its effects, seemed to work. It started in July and by October she was ready for the planned mastectomy. Despite contracting an infection, she recovered well from the operation and by Christmas she was getting back to normal. We were very hopeful of a cure.

At Christmas we celebrated her 60th birthday – she was born on Christmas Day. The family had prepared a 'This is your life' video for her. We had planned to do

In Manchester 1997

this before we knew about her illness. In the event, it proved to be doubly appropriate. We were able to gather together contributions from all aspects of her life, including her godmother in Leek, and people from every church to which we had belonged. Stephen and the others put it together and 'top-and-tailed' it with touching personal contributions from themselves. She just loved it – and so did we as we shared it together. We had all gathered at Stephen and Tricia's house for the season itself and had a lovely, precious time.

While we were there in Thornbury, Tricia gave birth to their second child, Naomi. Frances had simply loved being a grandma since Connor had been born two and a half years earlier, and to be there to welcome Naomi at the time of her birth was an added joy. The baby had been expected on December 23. When she did not arrive we wondered whether the birth might happen on Christmas Day, but it was not to be. Naomi kept us waiting until New Year's Eve!

Soon after Naomi's birth Frances and I returned to Manchester. My birthday present to her was a weekend in a luxury hotel in the Lake District. She wasn't strong, but she coped with it and thoroughly enjoyed it – as did I. Later in January, however, on a routine visit to the hospital, an abnormality was discovered in her blood. To cut a long story short, the cancer had returned. Further chemotherapy was not successful, and on July 22 she died in the Christie Hospital.

Frances had often said, from the time when we first met onwards, that she was not afraid to die, and it was evident that she wasn't. She deeply regretted leaving us all behind, but I am sure she was ready for what was to come. Her final moments are worth recalling. She lay in a coma in hospital and we were all sitting round her. At one point Rebekah, who had flown in from the States just in time, watching her, said: 'I do wish she'd go, don't you?' to which Judith replied: 'I bet I know what she's thinking: why don't they all go and let me get on with it on my own'. Soon after that she and the others left and I remained at the bedside. After a while I said a prayer and a blessing and kissed her. 'You are going on a journey' I said; 'Don't hang about!' Amazingly, she opened her eyes. What she saw, and what she was thinking, I cannot say. But it helps me to think that she was saying 'Everything's all right. I am content. Now go home'. So I did that; but I had not been in the house many minutes when the phone rang and the message was that she had gone. She had done what Judith had said she wanted to do, on her own, without any fuss. This was so typical of her and I am grateful for that last memory.

We had a funeral with a difference. First, the family and very close friends gathered at the South Manchester Crematorium to say goodbye, each of us placing a rose on the coffin before leaving. We then went for lunch at a restaurant she and her friends from Gatley Church used to frequent for evening meals together, and afterwards went to the Gatley church for a thanksgiving service. We had planned this service in considerable detail. It was taken by the recently inducted minister, the Revd Margaret Tait. It can now be revealed that it was in a conversation between Frances and myself that Margaret's name had first presented itself as a possible future minister for Gatley, and Frances had been involved, as a member of the congregation, in the process of Call. So it was doubly appropriate that Margaret should preside. Our very old friend from college days, the Revd Howard Starr, presented a lovely tribute which summed up Frances beautifully. Other friends took part by reading Bible passages and other readings they had chosen – Jean Gray from Plymouth, Peter Linsey whom we first got to know in Cardiff, Betty Frank our friend from Sussex, Daphne Clegg from Palmers Green, Kath Archer from Gatley, and the Revd Michael Hodgson, a neighbouring minister who had visited Frances many times during her illness. A version of the song 'Give me joy in my heart', written by Paul Bateman of Palmers Green, was played on tape, as was Andrew Lloyd Webber's 'Pie Jesu', and the congregation sang full-heartedly three hymns: 'All praise to our redeeming Lord', which we had sung at our wedding; 'Have faith in God my heart', a particular favourite, sung at the funerals of both my parents; and 'God is love let heaven adore him', with its particularly appropriate couplet:

'And when human hearts are breaking under sorrow's iron rod
That same sorrow, that same aching wrings with pain the heart of God'.

Despite the sorrow to which that hymn refers, and because of the sense of joy and hope with which it concludes, the service was an amazingly uplifting experience. People had come from far and wide and packed the church to overflowing. The support of so many from the North Western Province and from other places where we had lived and worked was wonderful to experience. Frances would have been amazed. Never coveting the limelight, she had always tried to live her life out of the public eye. But it was evident from things that people said and wrote that she had had a profound influence for good on many, many people. Even during her illness, when she seemed to develop a new serenity of personality that radiated to all who visited her, she was still spreading her own characteristic kind of loving around. As is often the custom these days, we requested gifts of money instead of flowers at the funeral. We were astonished, and Frances would have been astounded, that around £6,000 were raised in this way. As a family we decided to set up a small trust fund, the income of which could be used to support charities in which she had been interested. Over the years the principal beneficiary has been a child we have sponsored in Ghana. We believe Frances would have approved of that. We scattered her ashes the following April at Bodnant Garden in the Conwy Valley, at a spot where she loved to sit. I visit this beautiful place from to time and feel as close to her there as I do anywhere.

I have written at length about this period of our lives in a little booklet entitled 'One whom I love has died', published at the beginning of 1999, so will not repeat it here. To say we found the parting terribly hard would be an understatement. Our lives can never be the same again. But each of us, in our own way, has picked up the threads of life and got on with living, as she would have wished. A big regret is that Frances had only a brief relationship with Connor and Naomi and never knew Sahara, or Stella, or Beau. She had longed to be a grandmother and would have loved watching them grow and sharing their lives. But it was not to be. As for me, I continue to live alone. When asked if I wanted her wedding ring removed from her finger before her funeral, I declined, feeling then. as I still do. that I remain married to Frances for all eternity. I can honestly say that never a day goes by without my thinking of her. There is a real sense in which she has never entirely left me. Our marriage was not perfect – what relationship is? But we loved one another deeply and gave each other the mutual support married couples can give. I am less of a man without her, but a better man because of having been married to her for thirty-eight years. And when, at times, I feel lonely or downcast, I can hear her, in her ever-practical way, saying 'Come on. Don't be silly. Life is for living. Get up and get on with it'. And usually I do!

I was back to work in earnest by the beginning of September 1998, realising that I had but twenty-two months to go to retirement. At times people remarked that I was probably beginning to 'run down'. My response was that I seemed to myself to be still running up – seeking to complete as many assignments as possible in the time I had left.

In the Spring of 2000 we moderators went to Brussels to visit the European Parliament and to meet the officers of the Conference of European Churches. It was a fascinating visit, convincing us of the importance of the European Union and its structures. and giving us an insight into the work and influence of Christian leaders within it.

A few weeks later I joined a United Reformed Church pilgrimage to Israel/Palestine, designed to celebrate the Millennium. I was particularly keen to go because the other Moderators and their spouses had been there for a study tour in 1998 when Frances had been too ill for us to contemplate the trip. This was a life-changing experience, I think, for all who went. Our tour guide was a Christian from Bethlehem, Ibrahim Jaber, who gave us a fascinating insight both into the classic sites associated with Jesus and the beginnings of the Christian Faith and, perhaps more importantly, into the political situation as it then pertained. We met a wide range of people, both Israeli and Palestinian, and stood amazed at the complications of the situation and the difficulty of seeing any resolution. Soon after we had been there the second, and long-lasting, intifada began, culminating in a horrendous wall being built by the Israeli government to seal off the two communities. I am sure that we shall see no lasting resolution of the problems of the Middle East until the Palestinian/Israeli interface has been justly resolved. But it has been going on in various forms for centuries – perhaps even from the time in the old Bible story of the twins Jacob and Esau struggling in the womb before their birth.

The current Moderator in Wales, the Revd Peter Noble, has a saying: 'He who aspires to be a Moderator deserves to be one!' Certainly this was a ministry to which I never aspired, despite Frances's comment to which I referred earlier. It is true, as Peter Noble's aphorism implies, that there is a huge down-side to it which one only discovers when one has embarked upon it. I found that I missed many aspects of local pastoral ministry: the leading of worship and preaching regularly in the same congregation; the day by day pastoral relationship to people; the deep involvement in a particular community. The work-load of a Moderator was also often heavy and sometimes excessive. But for all that, I found this ministry to be an enriching experience and one to which I look back with satisfaction.

When I came to retire, in June 2000, the Synod arranged a service of celebration in the cathedral in Blackburn, where we had held a Synod event on a summer evening a year or two earlier. The announcement of the event amused me: 'Our moderator is about to retire and a thanksgiving service will be held'! It proved to be one of those 'out-of-this-world' events. The cathedral was crowded. My family were there. People had come from my previous pastorates and from many of the churches in the Synod. A previous Moderator of General Assembly, Mrs Ruth Clarke, presided as the current Moderator, the Revd Peter McIntosh, was unwell and could not attend. Michael Hodgson, mentioned above, played the organ. The Revd Michael Storr, the Synod's minister of music, assembled a huge choir which sang Vivaldi's 'Gloria' and Rutter's 'The Lord bless thee and keep thee' – pieces that had been sung at my induction eight years before, and which now had even deeper meaning for me and for the congregation. The Revd Alan Gaunt wrote a special hymn for the occasion. I preached the sermon. A good friend within the Synod, the Revd Nigel Uden, led prayers of thanksgiving and intercession. The ecumenical officer from Greater Manchester, Sister Maureen Farrell, spoke on behalf of the other denominations with whom I had worked. The Synod Clerk, Raymond Clarke, led a number of people, including the Bishop of Blackburn, in a simple act of completion and dismissal. I was presented with a large cheque, and – a nice touch – each of the seven District Councils in the Synod presented me with a symbol of my ministry, just as they had presented me with symbols of their life at my induction service. Among the gifts presented was a bound volume of pages of signatures from all the churches in the Synod – a gift I shall always treasure. It was a wonderful evening. And shaking hands at the door afterwards took as long as the service itself had taken!

I guess many people will recall one unscripted incident during the service. At one point I came round to the front of the congregation from where I had been sitting. Naomi, then two and a half, spotted me for the first time clad in my robes. 'Grandad's got a nice new dress on' she pronounced, loud and clear! It brought laughter from all who heard her, of course, and contributed to the family atmosphere of the occasion.

The following evening a reception was held in Luther King House in Manchester. Thus I retired surrounded by the appreciation and love of many people which I deeply and humbly appreciated, and still do. In the words of the Psalmist, 'The boundary lines have fallen for me in pleasant places' and very few of them, it seems, as the result of my own choosing!

Chapter 14
RETIREMENT? – 2000–

Where should I go to retire? Some people, when they reach this time of life, 'like exiles long for home'. I am unsure where 'home' is for me. Letchworth where I was born? Cambridge where I was brought up and went to college? Bristol? Plymouth? Cardiff? London? Manchester? I had lived in nine different houses in my lifetime but 'home' had moved with me. In each place I had put down roots, but had had to pull them up when moving. I toyed with the idea of moving back to Cambridge, the place where my deepest roots had been. But life moves on, and places change, and nothing is the same as it was. Increasingly I have come to think that one cannot go 'back' anywhere. Life is a pilgrimage for me, settling down for the time being where I am meant to be, but travelling on from time to time. Had Frances lived, we'd probably have remained in the Manchester area. It had proved to be a very pleasant city in which to live, and it held many delights we had hardly begun to explore. Frances, for her part, had begun to develop her own life independent of my calling. She had trained and worked as a Samaritan, and enjoyed this very much. She had also become a magistrate on the Manchester Bench and was beginning to find this very rewarding. And she was enjoying her daily work at Luther King House and planned to continue it at least until she herself would reach retirement age. I had said several times that she would have followed me around the country for 40 years, so it would be for her to choose where we would go to retire. Had she lived, I guess we'd have sold our house in Old Colwyn and bought one in Gatley where we were happily members of the church; she'd have continued with her activities and I'd have found something to do which I would have found congenial.

But things were now different. I suppose the ministry is one of the very few professions where it is advisable for people to move away from their sphere of work when they retire. For most other people the advice is, 'stay where you are, where your friends are, where your interests are, where you are at home'. But for ministers it is different. I have seen too many ministers who remain where they have served, causing anxiety to their successors by being unable to take a back seat, to think it is good for them to remain in the locality. So, when I found myself alone, I felt that

I should take a dose of my own medicine and move out of the province. I already owned a house – in Old Colwyn. Should I go there? I vividly remember a conversation in mid 1999 with the Revd John Humphreys, then moderator of the Wales Synod. 'What are you going to do when you retire?' he asked; 'are you coming to live in Old Colwyn?' In reply I heard myself saying: 'I think I could only live in Old Colwyn if I had something specific to do' - a foolish thing to say to a moderator, as I should have known! The next month he was back: 'What about being half-time Training Officer for North Wales?' I agreed with his suggestion, wrote my CV, and attended an interview in Cardiff. At the end of the interview, the chairman Dr Alun Jones, said, quite properly, that, having been and discussed the matter with them, I should go away and think carefully about it, and, if I felt on reflection that the job was not for me, they would understand. 'But' said the Revd Nanette Lewis-Head, a member of the interviewing group, 'we shall be very disappointed!' - not the kind of remark people in interviewing groups are supposed to make, but I did not disappoint them – at least at that stage! I accepted the invitation, yet another totally unsought Call, and, having spent some money Frances had saved for our retirement on upgrading the house, I moved to Old Colwyn in August 2000. In the October of that year I was inducted to my new ministry at the autumnal meeting of the Wales Synod.

I have not regretted the move or the work I undertook. Old Colwyn has proved to be yet another very pleasant place in which to live: enough life and activity to keep me involved, while at the same time having a slower pace than the cities in which I have previously lived. 'Grandad's little house', as a plaque in the porch given to me by Connor and Naomi when I moved in says, quickly became just right for me – not large, but large enough both for one person on his own and to provide accommodation for visitors when required. At a pre-retirement course which I attended in Windermere it was spelled out that we should carefully consider several criteria when looking for a retirement home: the house should be on level ground, within walking distance of shops, with a main trunk route not too far away, a good bus service, a nearby railway station, a good doctor's surgery, a general hospital not far away and a local Church to which to belong. Amazingly, this house fulfills all those criteria! Its only drawback is the distance from the family. But Frances and I always said we'd not want to move to be very near any one of them lest they should move away and leave us stranded or, alternatively, might feel unable to do so because we had moved there. In any case, with two children in different parts of London, one in the South-West and one in New York, it would be hard to decide where to bestow myself to be near them. Britain is not a large country, the transport links are good, for senior citizens the buses are free for residents in Wales and rail travel is very reasonable for those with Senior Citizens' passes, so North Wales is in many ways as good as anywhere, offering as a bonus a wide variety of attractions for visitors of all ages. So here I am, and here I look like staying for the time being.

The work I did for five years after coming here undoubtedly filled a significant gap in my life. Had I retired and had nothing to do, being on my own, life would have seemed very empty. As it is, I moved into new work, with new colleagues in a new place. Thus, when for many people life begins to narrow down, I have found that new opportunities have opened up and I am very grateful.

I had not expected to return to Wales. When we left in 1976 I remember saying to Frances in the car as we crossed the Severn Bridge into England, 'We've had one pastorate in Wales and we don't need to have another'. Yet here I am back again – admittedly in another part of the principality, but back all the same. Wales is a different place from what it was thirty years ago – more self-consciously a distinct nation, yet more welcoming to incomers like myself. Devolved government, for all its drawbacks, has been a positive development, helping to give a sense of nationhood. But Wales remains, and I think always will remain, heavily dependent on the rest of the UK for its present life and future development. The United Reformed Church in Wales exhibits the same dependency. We are the 'National Synod of Wales', known thus since the United Reformed Church's unification with the Congregational Union in Scotland in 2000, the Churches there becoming the 'National Synod of Scotland'. We differ significantly in many ways from the eleven English synods: the 'WID' factor, as it is known: 'Wales Is Different'. One way in which we are very different is in the size of the country we cover – larger than any of the English provinces by far – and the smallness of our membership: now only about 3,500, spread out over 118 churches, many of which are very small and thinly scattered. On our own I doubt if we could survive at all. Integrated into a Church in three nations, we are able both to maintain our common life with them and to develop our distinctive witness. Many of our ministers are English – only about half a dozen of the thirty-plus serving in Wales are themselves Welsh. It is evident that, even at this level, we need our English brothers and sisters. Financially too we receive more from central funds that we contribute. We are not unique in our weakness. Most of the other mainline denominations in Wales could tell a similar tale. Those that do not straddle the border – the Presbyterian Church of Wales and the Church in Wales – are in a precarious state. Indeed, church life as a whole in this principality is at a low ebb. I lead worship Sunday by Sunday principally in United Reformed and Presbyterian Churches. In few are there any significant numbers of children, in many none at all. There are towns in Wales where there is not one child in any of the churches. In some places, at 73, I am the youngest person in the congregation. One feels sympathetic with those who remember better days, albeit sometimes looking at those days through rose-tinted spectacles. They have faithfully kept the show on the road for all these years and now see their beloved church gradually fading away before their eyes. There are some exceptions to this picture, and I thank God for them, but this is the general pattern of church life into which I have entered.

I do my best to offer words of hope and affirmation and to help where I can. For the first time in my life I find myself a member locally of a little church of about 15 members. They are a loyal and committed community and took me to their hearts when I arrived. Their average age, however, is high – only three members are still in paid employment - and there are no young people or children. The time must surely come when their future must be addressed. Meanwhile I serve them as best I can as an elder, but am inevitably an infrequent worshipper as I get many invitations to lead worship in other places. I could be doing this somewhere every Sunday if I allowed myself to do so. As it is, I book up every other Sunday, but often an additional invitation to undertake an attractive assignment or to help out in an emergency comes my way, so that I am worshipping in my 'own' Church no more than once a month. From time to time I am invited to travel further afield to lead worship. Ten or a dozen Churches in the North Western Synod have graciously invited me to return to my old stamping ground. Others in other parts of England have occasionally asked me to preach on special occasions, and on a couple of occasions I have re-visited Palmers Green at their invitation. So even at the level of leading worship I am not idle. I suppose I shall know when it is time to give up – I shall cease to receive invitations to preach! But meanwhile, I continue, partly because of the need of the churches and partly, if I am honest, because I love it and still feel called to do it.

In addition to preaching, for five years I carried out the responsibilities of my appointment as Training and Development Officer for the northern part of Wales to the best of my ability. This included helping ministers with their in-service training, offering training opportunities to elders, giving oversight and help to aspiring lay preachers, managing the United Reformed Church's lay-training course in Wales, and helping local churches to discern and address their mission. All this inevitably involved a good deal of planning and committee work as well as attending the Councils of two Districts and the provincial Synod. It also involved considerable travelling, usually by car (I covered over 25,000 miles a year) but when I had to go to Cardiff for meetings using the (slow!) train. Quickly I discovered what I always ought, as a moderator, to have known – that there is no such thing as a part-time ministry. Our former General Secretary, the Revd Arthur Macarthur, who took up a part-time pastorate after he retired, once said 'The only thing about it that is part-time is the stipend', and so I found my work to be. At the same time, I know I did the work at a slower pace than that at which I had been working hitherto, and there was nothing like the same level of responsibility. And I was enjoying what I was doing.

I suppose the part of the Training and Development work that gave me the most pleasure and satisfaction, while enabling me to share what experience I had had in ministry down the years, was working with local churches to help to develop their mission. In some places I helped churches of different denominations to unite. In Llandudno the United Reformed Church united with the Presbyterians. In Colwyn Bay our congregation joined the Methodists. In Rhyl, where I was Interim Moderator for a time, two United Reformed Churches and a Presbyterian Church came together, As I helped these moves to take place I found myself writing constitutions for the new situations. I was also involved in writing a constitution for the North Wales District Council and others for ecumenical bodies. Had anyone told me when I came to North Wales that this would become a major part of my work I might never have come! But it has been good not only to write the enabling documents but also to have a share in developing the life and mission of these churches.

As Frances's illness and death cut across the time I spent in Manchester, so an episode in my own usually good health created a gap in my ministry in Wales. Towards the end of 2002 it was discovered that I had leaks in two of the valves to my heart and an operation was advised. The nearest hospital that undertook such an operation was the cardiothoracic unit at Broad Green, Liverpool. After an angiogram there in May 2003 I entered the hospital in December and had the operation on 17th. As I lay on the trolley waiting to go into the theatre, having received the injections in my hands that took me under the anaesthetic, I remember thinking 'If I die under this operation, it will be a lovely way to go – I shall know nothing about it'. But I came back! One faulty valve was replaced (by tissue from a pig, I understand) and the other repaired. I was in intensive care for 24 hours and then returned to the ward I had left. I have nothing but praise for the attention I received and the skill of those involved. It was a good experience – one that perhaps I could have used creatively if it had happened earlier in my ministry – and I learned a lot from it, not least the kind of ministry that is helpful, and the kind that is not helpful, to people in hospital contemplating and undergoing major surgery. I also formed, at first-hand, a very positive experience of the National Health Service to off-set the many negative stories that are bandied about. The good stories should be told.

Living alone, I needed somewhere to go to recuperate after leaving hospital. An earlier request that I might go to my friends Howard and Margaret Starr, who were now living in active retirement in the Wirral, was readily agreed, and two days before Christmas 2003 Howard fetched me from hospital. I was weak, but they gave me strength, and I felt entirely at home with them. I cannot adequately thank them for their friendship and hospitality. On New Year's Eve I felt strong enough to go with them to the home of their daughter and son-in-law and family to see the New Year in. Though arrangements had been made for me to leave if I could not cope with it, I surprised myself and them by being able to stay until after midnight. I was recovering rapidly. At the end of January I came home, and at Easter took up my work again. Since then I have not looked back, and am so grateful for this extra lease of life and for opportunities to make the most of it.

Early in 2001 the little United Reformed Church in Old Colwyn of which I am a member asked for my help to consider and review their mission in the village. One of the fundamental intentions of our small denomination is to foster wider unity wherever possible. Following this through, I encouraged the local church to make approaches to the other churches in the village (of which, truth to tell, there are too many: twelve for 6,000 inhabitants) to see if there were ways in which they might work together. Gradually we established a branch of Cytun in Old Colwyn – 'Cytun' being the Welsh version of Churches Together. [Another constitution to write!] At the time of writing I have just concluded my service as its President. This new body, now five years old, has organised a good many successful activities and has made its presence felt in the community.

Deriving from this initiative, I was soon elected President of Cytun Colwyn and District, but this proved to be a somewhat moribund body, serving too wide an area, and we took steps to bring its life to an end. In the meantime I found myself involved in helping to set up a regional branch of Cytun for the Conwy County Borough, designed to give oversight to more local ecumenical developments and to act as a channel of cooperation with the County Borough Council [yet another constitution!] I am the founder-president of this body. It has begun well and it remains to be seen whether it can adequately carry out the functions to which it has set its hand.

In addition to these interesting local developments I was asked to become Convener of the General Assembly's Pastoral Reference Committee and held the post from 2003–2007. I enjoyed this essentially confidential responsibility – and the regular meetings in London have enabled me still to feel part of the central operation of the Church, as well as providing opportunities to catch up with those parts of the family who live in the metropolis. I have also continued to serve as a Governor of Northern (theological) College and have found the ongoing relationship with the college in a period of transition very interesting and rewarding. In July 2007, however, I came to the conclusion that as that I am no longer in close touch with training or education I should retire from this involvement. I had done it for fifteen years and I miss it, as I knew I would. But I am sure it is right to make way for new and younger blood in this all-important work.

I agreed to act as Training and Development Officer for five years, which took me to the age of 70. As I approached that milestone I decided not to seek a renewal of the appointment. I had given a good slice of time and effort to the work, and I was beginning to feel that I was getting too old to contribute as a holder of that post should. I was also looking for a little more time for myself! I am thankful that the opportunity came my way and for all the new friends and colleagues it gave me. But I was ready to move on. It has been a source of great satisfaction to me that a much younger minister, the Revd David Salsbury, in his thirties, was appointed to take over from me and is doing a splendid job.

My 70th birthday in June 2005 was celebrated in great style. We arranged a lunch party for family and very close friends in a hotel in Thornbury, near to where Stephen and family live. It was splendid, and as I looked around the table I reflected

Keith's 70th Birthday, June 2005

that, had I not married, nine of the people in the room would never have existed. I hope the world is grateful! A few days later I was present at my last meeting as a member of the Synod Executive Committee in Cardiff, and found a balloon with '70' on it attached to my chair and a beautiful cake provided for us all to share. Then, back in Colwyn, I discovered that our minister, Kate Gartside, had arranged a surprise party at her home for members and friends of the churches in the area, getting me there under false pretences, using Howard and Margaret as under-cover agents! It was a lovely evening and I felt so gratified that they had wanted to do it.

I have always been interested in politics and, probably deriving from my origins in working-class non-conformity, my interest has always been in a radical direction. I don't think anything or anyone could ever persuade me to vote Conservative! My natural sympathies have always been with the Liberal Party, even when there were pitifully few Liberal Members of Parliament. I recall, for example, a time in the fifties when, under their leader Clement Davies, they had less that ten MPs.

There was a famous election when the results were announced on the radio with the refrain, time and again, 'The Liberal candidate forfeits his deposit', having come a low third in the poll. In the sixties there was not always the opportunity to vote Liberal – they did not put up in every constituency – so I usually voted for the Labour candidate. Since the formation of the Liberal Democratic Party in the eighties candidates have emerged almost everywhere and fortunes have steadily improved. Today, with 60 or more Members of Parliament, their representation is the highest I have ever known it to be. Whether that growth will continue remains to be seen. A current apparent revival in the fortunes of the Tories might encourage some who had voted Liberal Democrat to return to their former loyalty – we shall see. When I was a minister in pastoral charge I thought it wise not to declare my political sympathies but to try to help members of the congregation make their own political judgement. Recently, however, having retired, I have taken out membership of the 'Lib Dems' and will do what I can to support the cause.

Since my second retirement I have served two pastorates as Interim Moderator and greatly enjoyed the pastoral contact this gave. Some of the responsibilities I took up during the time I acted as a Training and Development Officer in Wales have followed me into my second retirement. I have also taken on the ministry of Synod Lay Preaching Commissioner and the task of Chairman of the Synod Trust. More locally, under the new structure of the United Reformed Church, brought into being in 2007, I currently serve as a Synod Elder for the North Wales Region. One aspect of ministry I have found myself able to offer has been to act as consultant to other ministers who come to see me, some of them quite regularly, to reflect on their work or to discuss difficulties. I hope to be able to maintain this ministry as it is evidently of help to those who come and it gives me considerable satisfaction. As long as I am needed, and as long as I can physically and mentally respond to requests and invitations that come my way, I hope to continue to serve the Church I love and to which I have devoted my life.

Chapter 15
YESTERDAY, TODAY AND TOMORROW

The seventy-three years of my lifetime have seen immense change, not to say upheaval, in the life of the world, the nation and the Church. I am told that there has been more change in this period than in the previous 2000 years and that the pace of change is accelerating. I can believe it.

The cataclysm of the Second World War, together with the tragedy of the previous one, ensured that the world of the second half of the century would be significantly different from the early years. Britain had always seemed stable and confident, sitting as it did at the head of a world-wide empire. When I was at school over half the world in our atlases was coloured pink! Now we have de-colonised and are a member nation with many others of the British Commonwealth, all with equal status. Since the early 1950s comparatively free movement within that Commonwealth has brought a wide variety of residents to our shores, enriching our common life but also causing disturbance and unsettlement. Meanwhile another great empire of a different kind, ruled from Moscow, has collapsed, while a new 'commonwealth', the European Union, has become established – again I believe to the great benefit of all who are involved but also with strong tensions, potential disagreements and bureaucratic complications. The 1990s were a positive and hopeful decade for the world as it prepared to celebrate the millenium. Sadly, the event that is now universally referred to as '9/11', the terrorist attack on the World Trade Center in New York, has changed all that and we are aware that we live in a very unstable world. In my youth the great threat looming over us all was 'The Bomb', horrifyingly revived in our memories today as our government proposes to replace the nuclear submarine 'Trident'. The more immediate threat now is that of terrorism, exacerbated by the uncertainty of when and where it will strike. The other great cloud hanging over the future of the planet is global warming. Hopefully the leaders of the nations will be able to address this purposefully and unitedly before it is too late for the human race. It will not greatly affect my generation perhaps, except superficially, but my grandchildren will certainly be affected. Meanwhile the 21st century world is dominated by the United States of America, the only remaining so-called 'super-power', behaving as if the world owed it unconditional allegiance, governed at the time of writing by an obstinate president of limited ability supported by a dangerously right-wing version of the Christian Faith and a group of ruthless people of ominous influence and intention. The signs for the peace of the world are not propitious.

Our own land has also changed significantly during my lifetime. In Letchworth before the war one never saw a non-white face. Even in Cambridge, with a strong international element within the university, black and brown faces were conspicuous by their rarity in the forties and fifties. That is still the case here in North Wales and in some other parts of Britain. Not so in London, Birmingham, Manchester and the post-industrial towns and cities of the Midlands, Lancashire and Yorkshire. There are schools in some of our cities where literally scores of different languages are the first language of some pupils. Race riots have scarred the life of these communities from time to time. Interracial and inter-religious tension have become endemic in some places. All this is a challenge to our political parties and their leaders. There have been many honest attempts, in all parties, and by a myriad of voluntary organisations, to provide creative policies and positive leadership. After a long period of Conservative rule, the tables were turned in 1997 when Tony Blair and his New Labour Party swept the board. The party has remained in power ever since: a longer period of service than that of any previous Labour administration and undoubtedly an historic achievement. This government has made a strong contribution to the development of the common life of the nation and I would hope that its achievements will never be forgotten. Sadly, however, their tenure of office has been dominated by the highly controversial invasion of Iraq, undertaken as a flagrant act of aggression by Britain and America, flouting the will of the United Nations, more than half the world, and a large proportion of the citizens of this country. My daughter Judith took part with upwards of a million others in a massive protest march in London just before the invasion took place, but all to no avail. The aftermath of that war seems set to be with us for many years yet and no solution to the unrest it has caused has yet been found. It is difficult to avoid the impression that in this matter, as now in many others, we were governed for ten years by a highly intelligent, charismatic, but arrogant Prime Minister who listened to few people and insisted on his own way. This is little short of a tragedy, when it is remembered that he and his party came into power with a huge majority (probably too large for their own good) and immensely high hopes. What was that someone said about all power corrupting, and absolute power corrupting absolutely? Now we have a new Prime Minister:

Gordon Brown, a 'son of the manse' as he keeps reminding us, a man of perhaps more personal sense of principle than his predecessor. Time will tell whether he leads well or whether pragmatism takes over as it does for so many leaders. There was much talk, when he first took the reins, of him calling a snap election to elicit a mandate for his premiership. He did not succumb to that pressure and took a good deal of stick for not doing so. Personally, I saw now reason why he should do so. In this country we do not elect a Prime Minister, in the way the Americans elect a President. We elect a government, to be led by whomever is the leader of the party in power. I hope it will always be so.

The common life of our nation seems at the moment to be characterised by affluence, consumerism, acquisitiveness and other aspects of human selfishness and greed. The under-side of this, despite great attempts to eliminate it during the last ten years, is persistent unemployment among a comparatively small but significant section of the population, an increase in the number of people living 'below the bread line', a sense of powerlessness among some sections of the community, and a consequent acceleration of lawlessness, violence and crime. Community leaders and politicians wring their hands and search for causes and solutions. There is no way to prove it, but my hunch would be that a contributory factor to this state of affairs is the decline of the influence of religion and the virtual disappearance of the Sunday School and similar Christian organisations where children learned the fundamentals of right and wrong and wholesome living. On the other hand, there are very many good people around who are undertaking a vast range of positive activities in our society. The achievements of some young people, academically, in sport, in the arts and in community service, are astonishing and incredibly gratifying. Movements designed to enhance the life of the world community are well supported and moderately successful: people seeking to establish fairer trading patterns and thus bring about a just world economy; others working to preserve the environment; others involved in Voluntary Service Overseas; yet others caring for disadvantaged and marginalised people at home. The picture, though different from half a century ago, is by no means as bleak as some prophets of doom sometimes suggest.

The Church in the UK has seen inexorable decline in attendance, though not necessarily in influence, during my lifetime. The United Reformed Church, of which I am still proud to be a minister, has declined from 192,000 adult members at its inception in 1972 to 73,000 today, while the number of children worshipping on a Sunday has reduced from 102,000 to a mere 18,000. Against these figures must be set an uncounted number of adults who attend worship, sometimes during the week, who have not sought membership, and about 60,000 children involved in Pilots and uniformed organisations who do not usually attend on Sundays. The trend is nevertheless steadily downwards and the average age in most churches is high. We are also experiencing a good deal of negativity and, indeed, opposition from atheist writers, broadcasters and politicians who not only ignore or even scorn us and all we stand for, but set out with almost evangelical fervour to secularise the community and reduce the influence of religion of all kinds. The picture of decline is similar in churches of most denominations, despite a good many positive and hopeful pictures in some places and the existence of some churches that appear to buck the trend. When people of my generation were ordained we knew the Church even then was declining. Older people used to talk wistfully about the large congregations of their youth, or of the flourishing youth activities in which they were then engaged, and of a personal life that seemed to revolve almost entirely around the church. We knew the Church was getting smaller, but I don't think it ever occurred to us that when we came towards the end of our ministries people might seriously be talking about the extinction of the Church as we knew it. Now, there are times when we seem to see the Church we have loved, and to which we have given our lives, steadily evaporating before our eyes. It is a sobering prospect. I have enough confidence in the grace of God and in the power of the love of Jesus to believe that, to quote Pastor John Robinson's words to the Pilgrim Fathers in 1620, 'The Lord hath yet more light and truth to break forth from his holy Word', but just where the good Lord is leading his Church in the western world at the present time is hard to discern.

In the early years of my ministry ecumenical fervour was evident. Some of us paid considerable attention to what the World Council of Churches and the British Council of Churches were saying and doing. I remember waiting eagerly for reports from world Assemblies and the ecumenical lead I knew they would give. In my mind's eye as I write I can still see the covers of printed reports from the meetings in New Delhi, Uppsala, Nairobi and other significant world gatherings that took place in the sixties and seventies. Meanwhile, as a minister of the Congregational Church I was proud to be part of the process that led, in 1972, to the formation of the United Reformed Church. I shared the eager hopes of many that our united action might pave the way for further acts of union within my lifetime. Other denominations, however, were not prepared to respond to the lead we hoped we had given, and organic union slipped off the agenda of the Churches. In the 1980s Churches Together in Britain and Ireland was formed, and the emphasis came to be placed on united local action rather than organic union. This is all very well, and it works where people are enthusiastic, but it is a process from which any congregation can easily opt out if it wishes. From where I sit at the moment the ecumenical picture is not rosy. It is difficult to see where it can lead until we grasp the matters of contention between the different denominations more purposefully than we have in the past and make new moves towards inter-denominational union. I still cherish the hope that the Churches might return to this search, though in the present 'ecumenical winter' as it has been called it is difficult to see many green shoots. My father used to say that the first step towards a united Church was to be a good member of your own denomination, to know what it stands for, to appreciate its strengths and weakness, and thus be prepared to share with others the gifts God has given to that denomination in its time of separation. The next step was to be willing, in all humility and openness, to take on board the gifts God has evidently given to those in other traditions. Thereafter, in creative encounter, as people of different persuasions took each other seriously and learned from each other, organic union would be self-evidently the only possible way forward. I have always tried to follow this advice. It has led me into all kinds of complications at times, as might have been seen in what I have written. But I wonder whether people today know enough about their own denomination, and are confident enough in what it stands for, to be able to follow the same advice – and whether this is one of the factors that influence the general lack of interest in the search for unity. Indeed, my observation is that most Christians are not interested in the wider life of their own denomination, never mind other denominations. Most local churches, whatever their designation, are basically congregational in outlook.

The United Reformed Church has suffered more drastically than most in the spiral of numerical decline. Perhaps a contributory factor is that we suffer to some extent from a lack of distinctive identity. This is understandable when one remembers that at our inception we were seen as a movement to unlock the ecumenical log-jam. Few of us gathered in Westminster on October 5 1972 thought that we would still exist as the United Reformed Church thirty-six years hence. Our raison-d'être was to lose ourselves into something altogether more comprehensive, thus enhancing the mission of the Church in the UK. That this has not happened has left us standing on one leg, with no obviously distinctive role. I sometimes wonder whether we shall continue to decline until the ecumenical climate changes. If and when that does happen, however, we shall need to be there, ready to share our ecumenical vision and experience and to discharge the calling that has been ours all these years. I pray that we may be.

Meanwhile the United Reformed Church is currently involved in a time of review, analysis and planning under the title 'Catch the Vision'. The hope is that, rather than being mesmerised by decline, we should rediscover our commission and our 'core values', turn around and concentrate on becoming an authentic witness to the Gospel and a valid instrument in its service, notwithstanding our small size and declining statistics. We are also using the opportunity to slim down our national structure. I pray that this process may succeed. There are signs that it may. As the so-called 'glory days' of the Church in this country disappear over the horizon for ever, taking with them the last vestiges of the power and influence we once had, and as we let that happen, maybe we shall discover again the meaning of being called to be people of God, salt, light and leaven in the life of the world as Jesus called his little band of disciples to be. I retain the faith that God is still God and that, as our General Secretary Dr David Cornick has said, 'God has not finished with us yet'.

Thoughts of decline and apparent failure came into my mind as I lay in hospital in Liverpool in 2003. Since I had been ordained the Church had shrunk to half its size, the numbers of young people and children (with whom I had always loved to work) had reduced catastrophically, the ecumenical journey, to which I had very early committed myself, seemed to have run into the sand. What effect had my ministry had? What had it all added up to? Had I and people like me hitched our wagon to an illusion? I began to be depressed, unusual for me. But then shoals of supportive cards and phone messages arrived, people visited, and I was surrounded by the love of people with whom I had ministered over the years. And I realised how important was the caring fellowship of which I was a part, and how precious it was to me, and therefore presumably to all who belonged. And I remembered Baron Von Hugel's dictum: 'Christianity is caring; caring matters most'. And my life and ministry began to seem worthwhile after all.

Ministers are ordained to 'the Ministry of Word and Sacraments and Pastoral Care'. The last of these, arising out of the other two, is of vital importance. I guess, however, that many ministers, myself included, struggle with it. When I entered the ministry there was a popular conception that ministers spent their mornings in the study, their afternoons visiting and their evenings attending a meeting or two. This was the model we aspired to emulate, forgetting that life is much more complicated today. It was the round of visiting that gave many of us a guilty conscience. It took me forty years to take on board the self-evident truth that the more visiting one does, the more (not the less) there is to do. Nor is all of it profitable, and, in the modern Church, with its multitude of demands on its ministers, not all of it is either desirable or necessary. My time working at Church House, involving tiring commuting, taught me that if one has been hard at work all day, and arrives home at about 6.30 for a meal, one doesn't necessarily take kindly to the minister calling, unannounced, in what is left of the evening. There are more ways than one of carrying out 'pastoral care'. For what it is worth, the pattern I developed was this. On arriving in a new pastorate, I would make it a priority to get to know the members and adherents of the church individually. I would then visit those in hospital and those who were housebound with some degree of regularity. I would also visit those who had requested a visit for specific purposes: to discuss a baptism, to prepare for a wedding, to make arrangements for a funeral, to discuss a particular concern. Where a visit was required I would usually book an appointment rather than call unannounced. I would also let it be known that I would be pleased for people to come to see me, provided they arranged it beforehand. Sometimes I would see people at the church. With such a policy I found pastoral work was usually manageable. More generally, I tried to cultivate an openness of attitude so that when there was specific need people would feel they could make an approach with ease. Despite all this, however, the list on the desk of those to be visited never seemed to diminish!

One consequence of the shrinking of the institutional Church has been the proliferation, in all denominations, of shared ministry and group pastorates. There are plainly not nearly enough ministers to provide one in every local situation, and even if there were the community could not sustain them. Ministry shared among a number of congregations is not new. I knew of it in my youth, particularly in rural areas. But it is much more prevalent today. Methodism has always known it, where a given number of ministers have always served a circuit – usually fewer ministers than the number of churches in any given circuit. In Wales the situation has become critical in some denominations. It is not unknown for ministers of the Presbyterian Church of Wales to be called upon to serve ten or a dozen little churches spread over a wide area. Such ministry, it seems to me, is self-defeating, particularly in the face of congregational expectations which tend to be traditional. It can only seek to maintain the status quo and can do very little by way of mission development. There are places where the United Reformed Church is not far behind its sister denomination in ministerial provision. All this requires a new understanding of the place of the minister within the community and the greater use of the leadership talents of those within the congregation who are not ordained. Paradoxically, this state of affairs has come about when those very talents are in shorter and shorter supply. It is difficult to see how this situation can be resolved. Congregations seem set to continue to decline, and ministerial availability to reduce even further. Myself, I have never been called to minister to a group of churches, though I would have enjoyed the experience. I have always had the good fortune to minister in single pastorates, and can see the real benefit in the traditional relationship between a minister and a congregation in terms of pastoral care and mission development.

Styles of worship have changed significantly during the 48 years of my ministry. I was ordained at a time when a minor revolution in liturgy was under way. Non-conformity in most denominations had been characterised by what was often irreverently known as 'the hymn sandwich'. The climax of worship was the sermon. My father's generation even called the hymns, readings and prayers 'the preliminaries'! The sacrament of Communion was observed no more than monthly, and then it was tacked on to the end of the 'preaching service', with a break in between during which a large proportion of the congregation often left. In the 1950s what became known as the 'Liturgical Renewal Movement' gained momentum and affected all denominations. Order and dignity came to be prized. Each part of the service was seen to have its proper place in building up a 'full diet of worship' and the Lord's Supper took the place it never should have lost, at the climax of the act of worship and integral to it. Some of the less acceptable practices of the former style still linger in some places, but the vast majority of churches show that they have been deeply affected by this movement. It interests me to note that the basic liturgical structure of worship in almost all denominations, from Roman Catholic to Methodist and all stations in between, is now very similar. The elements of Praise, Confession, Assurance of forgiveness, the Word read and then preached, Prayers of Intercession, Offering and Communion, usually in that order, are all there.

That said, there has continued to be change and development in the structure and content of worship. When I began my ministry Free Church worship was led almost entirely by the minister. Bible readings were normally read from the

Authorised (King James) version. Sermons were about 20 minutes long and sought both to proclaim the Gospel and to teach its implications. Apart from the times when the sacrament of Communion was included within the service, the whole act of worship was conducted from the pulpit and was characterised by order and dignity. To add emphasis to this, many of us ministers dressed ourselves in the full Reformed regalia of cassock and bands, gown and academic hood. Now, the leader of worship will often lead most of the service from a lectern at a lower level than the pulpit, sometimes but not always going to the pulpit for the sermon. Members of the congregation will read the Bible readings, which are almost universally from a modern translation. Sometimes they will also lead the prayers of intercession. The hymns will often be chosen from a variety of sources, and will reflect both the traditions of the Church and the output of the many contemporary hymn-writers. Prayers, particularly in a service of Communion, will frequently contain formal responses by the congregation. Sometimes, in some places, a great variety of method is used to present the theme of the service: drama, dance, film, discussion. Symbolism, in the form of crosses and pictures – even sometimes candles – will be evident. A recent development has been the introduction of PowerPoint whereby hymns and other material can be projected on to a screen at the front of the church to encourage participation. These innovations are not always accepted without opposition: 'If I had wanted a service like that I'd have gone to the Anglicans' is a comment I still hear from time to time, especially when responsive prayers are introduced. But the innovations have undoubtedly enhanced the corporate nature of worship, and the sense of it being offered not by the leader alone on the congregation's behalf but by the whole people of God in that place. I am very comfortable with these developments.

At the same time, there has been another influence at work within the life of the Church, spanning all denominations. I refer to what is usually known as the 'Charismatic Movement'. This is seen as a new outpouring of the Holy Spirit, leading to a loosening of restraint and an enhancing of spiritual life. In its more extreme forms this has led to astonishing manifestations and not a little division within the fellowship. In less way-out forms it has had a noticeable effect on the style of worship in many churches. The emphasis is on enthusiasm and informality. Modern songs of a particular kind are sung, often at great length and with much repetition. Traditional hymns are ignored. Times of prayer are informal, with much contribution from members of the congregation. Formal responsive prayers are out. Sometimes 'speaking in tongues' will take place. Sermons will often be long and discursive, frequently delivered by ministers walking around the church, carrying a large open Bible to which they refer frequently. Pulpits are ignored or removed altogether. The Lord's Supper will not always take place so regularly or so publicly as it does in more traditional churches. No ministerial robes will be seen. There will be much emphasis on 'the joy of the Lord'.

It is difficult to know where all this will lead, or how permanent a feature it will be seen to be within the Church. For my part, I am happy to accept that some congregations find this kind of worship suits their needs. I would hope they would give some attention to making it the best it can be within its own style, and not slipshod or disordered as it sometimes is in danger of becoming. I would also want to remind them of the centrality of the Sacraments within the Church. I cannot help resenting what comes across as arrogance in the attitude of some who espouse this way of worship, suggesting or implying that this is how the Spirit must manifest itself, and that those of us who are not attracted to this way of worship are somehow deficient in our experience of the Spirit. I am, however, obliged to accept that it is often churches of this kind that are growing. I would hope that, within a Church that seeks to embrace variety of gifts and understandings, different expressions of the Gospel could learn to live together within the one Body. That said, I have to say that, trained as I was and having had the experience I have had, I find worship of this informal nature less than satisfying, both as a leader and as a member of the congregation. I shall therefore continue to be 'me' – preaching gown and all!

Throughout my ministry the matter of the ordination of women has been a potentially divisive issue within the life of the Church. When I was a young minister, women were a rarity within our ranks. Out of over 30 students in house during my year at the Western College only two were women. Now about a third of the ordained ministers within the United Reformed Church, and more than half our students in training, are women – such is the change that has taken place. I believe we can take pride in the fact that the first woman to be ordained within the Congregational Union, Constance Coltman, was ordained as long ago as 1917, and I am delighted that Baptists, Methodists and Anglicans now ordain women, although, as yet, women cannot be bishops within the Anglican Church. There is pressure for female ordination even within the Roman Catholic Church, just as there is also pressure for priests to have the option of being married. I doubt, however, whether my generation will see this coming about.

A matter of some contention has been the use of inclusive language. The eighties were a time when gender came to the fore. Within the United Reformed Church, an Assembly resolution decided that in future all our publications would use inclusive language. That meant that the hymnbook 'Rejoice and Sing', published in 1990, and various service-books, came under this stricture and, wherever possible, exclusive terms like 'he', 'man', 'mankind', were changed. God, however, is often still referred to as 'he'. An amusing comment in the Assembly debate on this issue has gone down into folklore. The Revd Ron Williams, always an Assembly character, remarked: 'Gender? Gender? Moderator, we don't have gender, we have sex'! Thus put in its place, the whole issue has left the headlines and is now more or less accepted among us as a battle that has been won – though it still rankles with some on both sides of the debate.

Amid all the change that has been going on, in the Church and in the wider world, a particular issue has come to the fore: that of the rights of people of homosexual orientation. In the nation huge developments have taken place. In something like thirty years we have moved from a situation where homosexual practice was illegal, even in private, to one in which homosexual people have equal rights under the law and may now cement their relationships, if they wish, in a civil partnership. There are still, lamentably, incidents of discrimination and even of 'gay-bashing', but for the most part the new legal equality is reflected in community attitudes. The Church, however, has been slow to adapt to these changes, and there are many within the Church who still regard homosexual practice as condemned in Scripture and therefore unacceptable for Christians. Currently we are witnessing great division within the world-wide Anglican Communion on this issue and it is difficult to see how it can be resolved. The United Reformed Church debated the matter during the 1990s, focussing particularly on whether practising homosexual people could be ordained to the Ministry, but in 2000 we agreed to a seven-year moratorium on the issue. General Assembly in 2007 debated how we might move forward now that the moratorium had run its course. Thankfully, and largely due to a report presented by the Revd Malcolm Hanson (a former moderator known to take a conservative position on many matters), Assembly, by an overwhelming majority, accepted that there is a variety of view among us and agreed that we must walk forward in mutual respect, affirming one another's integrity, as we seek a common mind. I like to think that this conclusion, and the process by which we reached it, has something to say to other Churches which are tearing themselves apart over the issue. For myself, I stand with those who believe that a person's sexuality is decided by nature and not by choice, and that if a person is by nature homosexual, he or she must be accepted as a child of God, the object of God's love and grace. Those who seek to interpret Scripture literally, on this or any other issue, to my mind fail to reckon with the culture within which particular scriptures were written or with the overall thrust of the Bible that God is a God of love and acceptance. I therefore fully accept people whose orientation is different from my own and affirm their right to give expression to their sexuality within a committed relationship.

My theology has changed as the years have passed. As I have recounted in earlier chapters, I was heavily influenced in the early days by conservative evangelical thinking. I recognise that still today it is churches based on such theology which are showing confidence and often growing. But, as time has gone on, I have moved away from that position. I dislike and distrust labels, but I suppose my evangelical friends would put me in the 'liberal' camp, and that, I know, is unfashionable these days. For me, it is an honourable position to hold. Increasingly I see fundamentalism of all kinds, in all faiths, as the enemy of community cohesion and peace. I believe that faith must be accompanied by reason – that God gave us minds as well as hearts and expects us to use them. I believe the Bible to be unique as witness to the living Word of God, which reaches the zenith of its expression in the man Christ Jesus. I judge the Bible itself, and all other potential revelations of the mind of God, by the criterion of the revelation seen in him, the 'Word made flesh'. And I trust the Spirit of God as guide, support and strength for living. I believe that faith requires community to sustain it and to express it in action in the world, so I believe profoundly in the Church as an instrument of the Gospel. And as for the world, its present life and future prospects, I find tremendous affirmation in the simple words of Bishop David Jenkins when he was asked to express his faith in as short a sentence as possible: 'God is; God is as God is in Jesus; therefore there is hope'. The universe, and human life within it, presents more and more challenges to faith, but faith, I believe, can help us to live with the questions it poses. For years I have found support in the well-known dictum of Herbert Butterfield: 'Hold to Christ, and for the rest be totally uncommitted'. Increasingly this is what I try to do.

I acknowledge that I have had a pretty wonderful life. Pleasant places have been peopled by pleasant personalities. I have had a wealth of opportunities, more perhaps than many people, and have been enabled to rise to the possibilities in at least some of them. I might have been an architect. I might have been a teacher. But I would not have missed being a minister for the world. In all honesty I have to say that, even in periods of difficulty and stress, there is no other work I would have preferred to have done. The fact that I am still doing it, in a more limited way, is witness to that. Undergirding everything is the conviction that I was called to it and I could do no other than respond affirmatively, gladly and freely.

Regrets, generally speaking, are unhelpful. I do have some. In particular I regret being so committed to my work that the time I had available for my wife and children was limited and often rushed. The wife of a colleague minister has just written that the Church was always her husband's mistress. I hope that was not the case with me, but I fear it might have seemed so at times. Perhaps that is one reason why my children have moved away from the Church and play no part in it. If so, then that is a considerable regret. I do have a good relationship with them all, however, for which I am very grateful, so it cannot all have been loss. As for Frances, whom I miss so much, I do deeply regret that we were cheated out of time together in retirement, to which we had both begun to look forward, and therefore have not been able to do together all the things we had planned. There is a simple lesson in that: if you want to do something, and have the opportunity to do it, do not put it off: do it now. You never know how much time is left. But we cannot change the past it, good or not so good. We have to live with it, including any mistakes we might have made, and we can never know what life would have been like if we had made different decisions.

I am increasingly aware that my life is much nearer to its end than its beginning. I recall a conversation with an elderly minister in Manchester who was in hospital for what turned out to be his final illness. 'Life's a bit of a disappointment' he said; 'You set out in your youth with all kinds of ideals. You get your head down and get on with the job to which you are called. And before you know where you are, your life if over.' I sympathise with what he said. I remember my mother saying several times when I was younger: 'The older you get the quicker it goes'. And it certainly does! I was in my first pastorate for about five years, and I thought I had been there quite a long time. I have now lived in my present house for eight years and it seems like the day before yesterday that I came. I read somewhere, but have forgotten where, that someone has done some research into the reasons why time seems to go quicker when we are getting older. I suppose one reason is that we are more conscious that, as one senior minister once said in my presence, 'we are all on fixed contracts – we just don't know the date on which they are due to terminate'. I have no wish to die. I really do not want my life to come to an end. Life is still so good, and there is so much I still want to do, that I certainly don't want to go yet. More profoundly, if I am honest, I have always been afraid of dying. I confess that I am not one of those Christians who are utterly sure of a life beyond death and cannot wait to get there. I find it quite impossible to conceive of eternity, if indeed it exists, or of my place within it. It seems to me that here on earth we are completely encased in a world of time and space, before and after, and cannot imagine what life might be like without those constraints. The nearest I can get to conceptualising 'heaven' is to say that it is not a place but a state of being, that it can begin in the midst of life here and now as we develop a relationship with God and with others, and that it is eternal because God is eternal. So what lies beyond death I cannot tell. I was heartened to read the autobiography of the Revd Michael Mayne, late Dean of Westminster and a saintly man. He was approaching his own death which by then was imminent, and said that he did so 'with a mingling of sadness, anxiety, uncertainty and trust'. I guess I approach mine in just about that spirit, and in the faith that, to quote a favourite passage of mine from the apostle Paul, 'There is nothing in life or death that can separate us from the love of God.' And for however much time I have left I will go on living to the full where God has placed me and with the strength and faith that God has given me.

THE END OF THE BEGINNING